A PLACE TO BE SOMEONE

A Place to Be SOMEONE

Growing Up with CHARLES GORDONE

Shirley Gordon Jackson

Introduction by
Maceo C. Dailey, Jr.

TEXAS TECH UNIVERSITY PRESS

This book is typeset in Monotype Goudy Old Style. The paper used in this book meets the minimum requirements of ANSI/NISO Z39.48-1992 (R1997). ♾

Designed by Lindsay Starr

LIBRARY OF CONGRESS CATALOGING-IN-PUBLICATION DATA
Jackson, Shirley Gordon.

A place to be someone : growing up with Charles Gordone / Shirley Gordon Jackson ; introduction by Maceo C. Dailey, Jr.

p. cm.

Includes bibliographical references (p.) and index.

Summary: "Covers the years prior to Charles Gordone's geographical and psychological journey from Elkhart, Indiana, to central Texas. The first African American to win the Pulitzer Prize for Drama, Gordone grew up in a multiethnic family that never fit completely into commonly understood racial categories, shaping his and his siblings' identities"–Provided by publisher.

ISBN-13: 978-0-89672-635-2 (alk. paper)

ISBN-10: 0-89672-635-5 (alk. paper)

1. Gordone, Charles–Childhood and youth. 2. Gordone, Charles–Family. 3. African American dramatists–20th century–Biography. I. Title.

PS3557.O72Z74 2008

813'.54–dc22

[B] 2008014636

PRINTED IN THE UNITED STATES OF AMERICA
08 09 10 11 12 13 14 15 16 / 9 8 7 6 5 4 3 2 1

TEXAS TECH UNIVERSITY PRESS
Box 41037, Lubbock, Texas 79409-1037 USA
800.832.4042 | ttup@ttu.edu | www.ttup.ttu.edu

Cover and frontispiece photograph: The five Gordon siblings, 1939
(*front row, left to right*) Leah, Charles, Shirley (*back row, left to right*) Stanley, Cecil.
Courtesy of Alexander Tschumakow.

This body of work is lovingly dedicated to Susan Kouyomjian Gordone, the widow of my brother Charles Gordone; without her inspiration, perseverance, and understanding it could never have been written!

CONTENTS

ILLUSTRATIONS

TABLE

POEMS

ACKNOWLEDGMENTS

My longtime Indiana friend, Lauraine Kendall Holycross, for her untiring efforts to obtain photographs and news articles from the archives of the *Elkhart Truth* newspaper, the Carnegie Public Library, and various high school yearbooks; she has my heartfelt appreciation.

I want to thank members of Gordone's high school class of 1944 for sharing memories of the teenaged Gordone.

Thanks to Steve Wylder, columnist, and Arden Erickson, staff reporter, for helping verify certain materials and historical information from the archives of the local newspaper.

Let me also express my deep appreciation and gratitude to Gordone's Texas Amarillo and Panhandle friends, among them Rooster Morris, Frankie McWhorter, Lannie Fiel, Henry Real Bird, and the late Buck Ramsey, for their insightful memories, their music, and their love—so meaningfully shared: white, cowboy, and Native American alike.

To Debara DePriest for her many hours at the computer, a thousand thanks!

INTRODUCTION

Many years ago, I sat in a downtown Baltimore theatre watching the play *No Place to Be Somebody,* written by Shirley Gordon Jackson's extremely talented brother Charles Gordone, the first African American playwright to win the Pulitzer Prize for Drama for his play, which was the first off-Broadway production to receive such distinction. I had attended the play with a church group primarily to please my girlfriend, whose father was the pastor of that church, and I anticipated a somnolent evening. While young, impish love would not get its way in the pleasing lane, the memory of the evening stayed with me for a lifetime, owing to the play's incredible richness and meaning. The gripping power of the play and the audience's engagement and reaction were evident: so much so that people were responding by talking directly to the actors on stage, sometimes filling in lines—and, in one case, offering up expletives—as the play spoke to their visceral realities and concerns. Thespians were to be found all around me, on stage and in the audience, bringing the play alive in a vivid, organic manner—call and response.

I had largely forgotten the particulars of that remarkable evening until a few years ago, when I was asked to read and, subsequently, to write the introduction to Shirley Gordon Jackson's family and personal memoir, *A Place to Be Someone.* I accepted the assignment with alacrity. This would give me an opportunity to peer into the world that had created the playwright and, even better, to explore it through a female perspective and first-person narrative by another creative artist—musician and painter—and prescient soul I would soon have the pleasure to meet. Joy came the evening of the mail delivery and my eager delving into reading the manuscript.

In her compelling family autobiography and memoir, Shirley Gordon Jackson provides a sensitive, thoughtful, analytical, and excellent accounting of an African American family in a very problematic place—Elkhart, Indiana—during a rapidly changing American era spanning the 1920s to the present. The story starts as "family romance," and at first glance we seem invited in to witness a functional, cohesive African American family—a composite of many different nationalities and ethnic groups—determined to scale the barriers of bigotry and racism.

Events move quickly, however, to the more emotionally wrenching subsurface matters that turn on the American meta-narrative of race preoccupying the family and impacting identity construction and child-rearing. First there are the parents, both married previously (she, divorced; he, widowed): a dark-skin African American male who marries a light-skin female, a not-too-uncommon occurrence in the black community mimetically measuring its standards of beauty and advancements by those of white America. Shirley's father questions why God made him so ugly and black. He embraces his wife because she was "close (in appearance) to a white woman." The mother is never more happy than when someone mistakes her for white.

The father's repeated denigration of blackness and the mother's unfulfilled ambitions for a more accomplished life made for the "White Mask, Black World" phenomenon noted by Shirley and its constant refrain, underscored by the parents (especially the mother), that the children had to strive to be "somebody." The children's fragile youth prompted efforts indeed to be "somebody" in seeking parental love and approbation. That they saw this as *sine qua non* to being loved created conflict and confusion, both of which were manifested most significantly—though creatively—in the adult life of Charles Gordone, who took on an almost Ellisonian preoccupation to find a spiritual, emotional, and intellectual world of comfort.[1]

Charles (the leader of the other four children, including Shirley, his sage recorder of deeds) struggled to excel at everything, becoming a very good student and athlete. But in a symbolic moment, he cuts off the curly hair (white-like in its length) of his brother. Charles also has to endure the humiliation of not being validated by his white fellow athletes, who maintain their off-the-playing-field social segregation and separation from him. Life comes with still more complications for Charles as he is unable to maintain a relationship with a white girl, "his first true love."

In his youth, Shirley writes, Charles had dreamed of owning the goose with the golden egg. On another occasion, she informs us that their sister carved into a kitchen drawer "IHTND"—I Hate That N— Dad! As Shirley notes, all of this made for a "sacrificed childhood," especially with a mother who, very late in life, reveals dark secrets to her daughter of her own molestations as a child and proclaims that "God didn't make good on his promise." Shirley experienced her mother as a woman "starved for affection" and with a "need to suffer."

The seeds of development seldom shoot straight up for a young girl within this configuration of mother-daughter relationship; in sprouting, they frequently entwine mother and daughter in a lifetime of discussion and sometimes discord before the two can be reconciled as friends, for one has planted in the other the haunting and halting voice of caution and chaos. All of this is far from our generation's television viewing of the amusingly contrived, mostly minor, family conflict of *The Adventures of Ozzie and Harriet* or *The Cosby Show*'s Huxtables. All too many of us find triumph fleeting and travail constant in family life.

Shirley, in relaying her family story of meaning and wonderment, has an innocence and boarding-school-like charm in placing herself within the narrative: "So I kissed the rough bark, which to my imagination must have simulated a man's unshaven face with a beard, and immediately it became a lover's face touching mine. Oh, I thought, to have someone strong to hold me, to care for me! I kissed the tree repeatedly. Suddenly, I heard loud laughter. I looked up to see Charles herding Mother, Leah, Cecil, and Stanley to front-row, center-aisle places on the steps of the front porch. . . . I think Mother realized this play-acting was a subconscious desire for affection, of needing to feel there was something or someone stronger than me who would shelter and protect me . . . hidden away in a recess of my young mind I had already developed an intuition that the sheltering and the strength weren't going to come from my parents or family."

Shirley may raise ire and eyebrows with her observation that "[o]ur family's ethnicity sprang from a stock of Welsh, Irish, French, English, Jewish, Italian, Native American, and Black genes. Yet history, with the complicity of the academic world and the connivance of Jim Crow laws, has ignored the other components of our lineage and focused only on the Black, essentially by use of the blind and automatic categorization of the obvious misnomer 'African American.'"

While reading Shirley's family story, I began to recall and recontextualize many of the memorable scenes from Charles's play that touched so deftly on themes in African American life, past and present. *Time* magazine averred in its review, with kudos to Charles Gordone, that "here is a black panther of a play"—a salute to one of the remarkable black student groups I admired in the late 1960s! *No Place to Be Somebody* was billed as a "Black-black Comedy in Three Acts"—something else I appreciated, as the play used humor to point up the foibles of the human condition. Act II, Scene Three, in which the play's protagonist, Gabe, delivers a monologue, held special sway with me that night in the theatre. His words called attention to the duality brought before me innumerable times by my parents and especially by my sixth-grade teacher, world-renowned storyteller Mary Carter Smith—the "reaffirmation/denial" side of blackness, which we would face at some point in seeking to get ahead in a white/so-called integrated America:

Whiter than snow, yes!
Whiter than snow!
Now, wash me, and I shall be
Whiter than snow!
Now those clean-white people thought we were
Dirty-black people
So we grew up clean and keen!
And all of our clean-white neighbors
Said we had earned the right to go
Out into the clean-white world
And be accepted as clean-white people!
But those dirty-black people!
Those dirty-black people!
Were still angry, jealous and mean!
They kicked us and slapped us and spit again
Disowned us
And cast us out!
For at last they knew
We were not like our clean-white neighbors!
Most of all! We were safe!
Assured at last!
We could never more be
Like those dirty-black Niggers!
Those filthy, dirty-black Niggers!
Who live far away!
Far away, in hovels across the tracks!
Oh, wash me and I shall be whiter than snow![2]

Pathos, pain, confusion, double consciousness, self-hatred, sickness, and yet hope were all to be found in that monologue, which resounded so significantly with African Americans whose lives had spanned the periods of the trek to the North, the changes from segregation to so-called integration, and the dynamics of semi-acceptance by whites.

I could have added a few lines myself to Gabe's evocation, about my own black community, where we kids were told to tuck in our lips and let our noses be pinched to make them smaller, thereby escaping the believed-to-be-generic African phenotype. The psychological terrorism of our youth sometimes preempted the physical assaults, as we were told to hush, don't wear red, and never be caught acting like a "n—"! We as African Americans, however, did move more readily from invisibility to visibility owing to the *Brown vs. Board of Education* decision of 1954, and we even got to see on television our prominent leaders pushing for political and civil rights.

What about the human journeys from being nobody to somebody, however? Charles turned to drama and comedy to address this. Shirley embraces family memoir and a retrospective of the circumstances out of which the concerns and the creative play sprang. This indomitable brother-sister act commands our attention: Shirley, especially, who invites us into the theatre of consanguinity.

A petite, very pretty, and gracious Shirley Gordon Jackson has managed in her memoir to deal boldly with a racially constructed, conflicted, confused family and America—where to be black was to be a pariah of one sort or another. As she holds up the mirror to a bygone era, we rightly have cause to tremble, but must assuredly keep the faith that as we saw ourselves then we not see ourselves now—hiding behind racial walls or still driven to foolishness by the color question. It may not be a matter of the truth setting us free, as Shirley well knows, but it might give us a better understanding of the boundaries and pitfalls along the way as we move, hopefully, from childhood to fulfilling adult lives. When stretched to meet the exigencies of adult life, the sufficiencies of our youth all too frequently disappoint the soul and/or give way to paralyzing stress and strain.

So at what point do we confront our childhood past, stripped of illusions and the need for denial? Is this necessarily a good thing as we age? Do we want to talk about the things that ail us emotionally and psychologically? Do we address the pathology? Take issue with our places in the world in favor of seeing our possibilities? This is a challenge facing all of us, and the narrative of race has complicated it immeasurably—for blacks, for whites, and for those in between!

In this regard, Shirley stands "in-between" in several respects—she is an out-of-wedlock child fathered by a white man, something her mother revealed to her when she was fifteen years of age. Yet her "in-betweenness" is at once a profound and poignant story about the potential beauty of childhood, the shaping of values, and pathology, all within the context of the family that Shirley explores.

We do well these days to turn the spotlight more readily on families that span the gamut from the divine to the dysfunctional, spawning in children the range of talents and abilities that send forth the genius or the jailbird. The world of children is one filled with fears and fantasies, many inherited and many created owing to the dynamics, dyad, or singularity of the parental situation. Training, sternness, indoctrination, and molding all take center stage, as children are met with words of kindness—"There, you have got it"—or the troubling admonition, "You will never amount to nothing."

Other questions seep in for children of color—watch out, for you will soon find out that you are not white, and to survive you must emulate whiteness almost to the point of self-abnegation. Indeed, when I entered college, I was asked when I first discovered that I was black. Reflecting on this invariably conjured up some memory of a perverse act of white bigotry or cruelty in denying a person access to a school, church, or drinking fountain. Many of us scurried home in the aftermath of such victimization experiences to ask our parents to explain from whence such venom and hatred came. Who wanted to call up—as we were being asked to do in that college class—such disturbing and denigrating memories and moments of youth?

Yet Shirley does so, graciously, looking at the interiority of the family. Charles, her talented brother, looked at the exteriority of the society, seeking to move beyond the world Reverend Dr. Martin Luther King, Jr., describes so eloquently in his "Letter from a Birmingham Jail," of being "harried by day and haunted by night by the fact that you are a Negro . . . when you are forever fighting a degenerated sense of 'nobodiness.'"[3] Charles continued to run in the labyrinth of identity formation and designation until he finally came to define himself as being of "three races . . . five nationalities . . . a North American Mestizo."[4] He found solace with his wife and soulmate—producer, director, and writer Susan Kouyomjian—and they moved to Texas (where Shirley now lives) to explore "the land and peoples of his dream" and foster a connection to the cowboy legend, then personified by a soon to become friend, Buck Ramsey. After her own fashion, Shirley also defines her vantage point firmly without raising a ruckus.

Shirley's family memoir and Charles's play emanate from their vision of the range of realities and historical circumstances of African American life in America. Both Shirley and Charles are real and as recognizable as the drumbeat of Africa and the melodies of a Beethoven sonata, or, more precisely put, the New World Symphony of Dvořák. Identity construction, or the one handed to Shirley and Charles, became the first challenge for them: to synthesize their sense of Americanness with their Africanness to avoid the feeling of "nobodiness"! What happens, as in the case of Shirley and Charles, when children grow up in the believed openness of the North, in proximity to the white world (albeit still in the shadows) and, more problematic still, in a family where the color compass compounds the burdens of childhood and life in general?

Both sister and brother experienced the circumstances of "double consciousness," which the eminent and exceptionally well-trained

Harvard black scholar W. E. B. Du Bois addressed.[5] The fact is that all things African American—talent, history, culture, explorations, and even defeat—begin with, come back to, or result from expansion of the thought, writings, and life of the great scholar W. E. B. Du Bois. If Du Bois gave us the veritable framework of analysis and understanding of the meaning of being black in America, we find ourselves now examining the myriad ways the story and saga played out—the particulars. What inspires greatness? What inspires madness? What inspires and sustains the ordinary? What inspires transcendence? What inspires denial, at what cost?

Shirley's memoir and the play of her brother Charles reverberate more fully when considered amidst the backdrop of the 1960s, but they both should be read with an eye toward the modern meaning in race relations. We need to recognize that Charles's play came during one of the most memorable and pivotal epochs in American and global history. A sleeping giant awakened in America in the 1950s, after the horrors of World War II and the beginning of the promises that bigotry and poverty could be addressed and possibly rooted out. In the early 1960s, everything seemed possible, and we appeared to be on the path to the Promised Land. I witnessed it from my Baltimore Forest Park High School. We knew struggle was necessary and vigilance virtue, and we believed victory was soon to be ours. How quickly youth faded, the darkness of the dream took hold, and the concerns and fears of young adulthood drove us into either hiding or passivity of one form or another. By the time I graduated from college in the late 1960s, despite the brilliance of our leaders—the Kennedys, Malcolm X, and Reverend Dr. Martin Luther King, Jr.—a fear was enveloping the nation that something was indeed going very wrong, especially with the deaths of the aforementioned men.

Still, there seemed a glimmer of hope in the Civil Rights and Black Power movements and what they did to inspire so many others, nationally and internationally. Protests against the war in Vietnam, student demonstrations nationwide and globally, the "Poor People's March," solidarity movements—gays, women, Blacks, Chicanos, Native Americans, and Asians—and reform movements and self-determination actions of those here and in colonized regions abroad presaged periods of progress and the palpable "Power to the People" shibboleth. Youngsters born of the families and eras Shirley discusses took different paths, but as they matured they made possible many of the movements to effect positive social change.

A good book gives rise to important questions and requests, and the opportunity cannot be bypassed here. Charles Gordone's widow should be inspired to take up her pen and complete the circle, owing to her relationship with Shirley and Charles. Susan continues to hold Charles's banner high to the point of reification. No more fidelity to the memory of a deceased one and an accomplished person can be paid than that of Susan's to her husband, Charles. He and she, in real measure, are the reasons for Shirley's literary foray into the family history and background.

Charles, in Susan's view, has not been accorded all the attention he deserves, owing to the politics of drama and the implicit and explicit messages of integration and acculturation inherent in his thoughts and writings. Black power and Black nationalism, Susan laments, had no place for Charles, in the theatre or in life itself. On both stages, he has been pushed regrettably to the rear of the proscenium, she contends, neither being fully written into the textbooks nor honored appropriately by the black community.

It may take Susan's own reflections on her work and life with Charles to give us a fascinating romp and revisionist view into the multiracial aspects of American theatre, in an equally dramatic era in politics and life itself. Such a work might cause all Americans to revisit the potentially debilitating construct of racial identity. Susan offers a glimpse into Charles's thoughts by drawing attention to his quote: "You must find yourself in everybody and not fall into the polarizing traps of color, class, religion, and politics."[6] Some indication of Charles's thinking can be found in the census of 2000, where, as noted by historian Nell Painter, "of the 36,419,434 people reporting themselves as black or African American, 34,658,190 said they were only black; 1,761,244 (4.8 percent) said they were black in combination with another race. Those people were likely to be young and to live in the West."[7]

I have, also thanks to Susan, a photograph of a painting of Charles Gordone and Ralph Ellison—one of *No Place to Be Somebody* fame and the other of *Invisible Man* fame—standing together and conversing at a social event. We have no tape of the dialogue between those two significant literary figures, but I think Shirley's memoirs may be the best recollections of events shaping her and Charles's life—and, by extension, Ellison's—along the axis of race, as she too moves with dexterity and verve from the lower to upper frequencies so readily shaping African American life and existence.

This family memoir takes us on a welcomed odyssey that alternates from being calm to stormy, but also one foremost sublime in its beauty and fierceness for truth. Shirley Gordon Jackson gives us hope that a balm is to be found in Gilead.

NOTES

1. Rampersad, Arnold. *Ralph Ellison: A Biography.* New York: Alfred A. Knopf, 2007. This biography provides an excellent analysis of the life and thought of the writer, whose remarkable novel *Invisible Man,* with its Bledsoe's law of "keep this N— boy running," represents one of the most poignant themes regarding talented African Americans who sought to better their lot but were victimized by continued bigotry and racism.
2. Gordone, Charles. *No Place to Be Somebody.* Indianapolis, New York: The Bobbs-Merrill Company, 1969, p. 45.
3. King, Martin Luther, Jr. *Why We Can't Wait.* New York: Harper & Row, 1964, pp. 77–100.

4. See article in *Deadline Magazine,* Berkeley, California, July 12, 1982, cited in a letter from Susan Gordone to Maceo Crenshaw Dailey, Jr., December 14, 2007.
5. Lewis, David Levering. *W. E. B. Du Bois: Biography of a Race.* New York: Henry Holt & Company, 1993; *W. E. B. Du Bois: The Fight for Equality and the American Century, 1919–1963.* New York: Henry Holt & Company, 2000. Professor Lewis won two Pulitzer Prizes, the first scholar to do so, for a two-volume biography, his brilliant foray into the life and makings of the great scholar and activist Du Bois.
6. See Susan Gordone to Maceo Crenshaw Dailey, Jr., February 11, 2008 (copy in possession of author of introduction). Ms. Gordone explains that this statement by her husband, Charles Gordone, was made in an interview with Susan Harris Smith in 1988.
7. Painter, Nell Irvin. *Creating Black Americans.* New York: Oxford University Press, 2007, p. 388.

Maceo Crenshaw Dailey, Jr.
El Paso, Texas, March 2008

A PLACE TO BE SOMEONE

Prologue

. . . A Place . . .

ALMOST IN THE CENTER OF northern Indiana, close by the southernmost border of Michigan and about 120 miles east of Chicago, lies a small town called Elkhart. It is a beautiful place in spring, summer, and fall, but dismal and dreary in winter. Situated at the confluence of two rivers—the St. Joseph, which flows east-west, and the Elkhart, which flows south—it had gotten its name from the Indians, to whom the small island separating the rivers' flow appeared to be shaped like the heart of an elk. The area teemed with wildlife attracted by the abundance of water and shelter and the availability of food. Elk, deer, moose, a bear or two, raccoons, chipmunks, and squirrels, even beaver, seemed to know they lived in an earthly Garden of Eden.

The red fox staked out his claim in forest and field, while mink and otter roamed the river banks. A rainbow of birds, from flashing red cardinals and bluebirds, larks and mockingbirds, to hawks and wild geese, all heard the staccato drumming of woodpeckers conducting their daily drill.

An unsurpassed array of flowering trees created beauty on every hand, and thickets of berries and brambles offered food and shelter to both man and wildlife. How one nourished the other!

Early settlers leaving the eastern states followed Indian trails leading to the Midwest and saw this amplitude of natural resources. They instantly recognized the advantages of unlimited timber for building, rich land for farming, and an almost overwhelming natural water supply. And so they determined to go no further. What matter that the Indians already occupied the area? The white man was accustomed to taking whatever he wanted from the redskins by either fair means or foul, and the thought never occurred to him that this land could be shared. To pacify the Indians, treaties were drawn up, stating that the land the white man didn't want would belong to the tribes for

As long as the moon shall rise,
As long as the rivers shall flow,
As long as the sun shall shine,
As long as the grass shall grow.
Indian treaty terms

Today, the Indians' only legacy is evidenced in some placenames bestowed by whites on the very land they had purloined from them: Osceola, Mishawaka, and Wakarusa, to name a few, although many others are scattered throughout the state. Even the name *Indiana,* meaning "of the Indians," was a pitiful travesty: a mere play on words, something to help salve the white man's conscience over what little he really had left for the Native Americans.

This little town with its surrounding plains and fields had a lot going for it. With such a plethora of natural resources its desirability was guaranteed, and growth was inevitable. Dr. Havilah

Beardsley, coming from a wealthy eastern family, settled in Elkhart and platted out the city in 1836. He helped incorporate the city in 1858, thereby assuring his position as one of Elkhart's founding fathers. The foresight and business acumen of Dr. Beardsley led him to build the first grist, flour, wood, and oil mills; he then added a saw mill. The addition of a ferry to cross the rivers opened up trade possibilities with other communities.

After the first train came through Elkhart in 1851, the years from 1871 to 1889 showed tremendous growth by the railroads. When switching yards, a divisional terminal, and a roundhouse were established, the demand grew for a large labor market. Soon, nearly five hundred men were working in the big shop and the roundhouse alone.

Then came World War I, and more than a few workers went off to join in the fighting. In 1917, as part of the war effort and to replace those workers, recruiters were sent south to persuade Negroes and whites to come north to fill vacancies not only in the railroad system but in stores, businesses, and farmlands as well. Colored people moving to town who had no place to live were put up at the Alabama House, a ramshackle old building just off Mason Street, over by the New York Central Railroad's back shops.

With the coming of the railroads and the switching yards, the face of Elkhart was forever changed. The tracks, running east-west, effectively bisected the town, and so the new groups of colored people, mandated to live *south* of the railroad tracks, found that the yards and railroad tracks became, for them, a very real Mason-Dixon Line.

Grandfather Morgan was one of the lucky ones: Uncle Horace, Grandmother's half-brother, who was already a railroad employee, let him stay with his own family up on Sixth Street rather than at the Alabama House. Grandfather soon was employed by the New York Central Raiload. When a house became available at 423 Chapman Avenue, Grandfather, now with a regular job, was able to send for his wife and children to join him, becoming among the first ten colored families to arrive in Elkhart. This, I'm sure, was a welcome move, for during the first thirteen years of Mother's life, the family had variously lived in Martin, Tennessee; Columbus, Kentucky; and Hickman, Kentucky. On Chapman Avenue our grandparents lived in that same house for nearly fifty years. This was certainly a more stable environment for the whole family.

I would like to explore what living in Elkhart meant in terms of *our* lives, beginning with our parents, then our grandparents, and on to my brothers, my sister, and myself. What part did that particular environment play in our development? Certainly bigotry and prejudices accompanied the new arrivals. Did our ethnic backgrounds manifest themselves in different ways in our genes, in part due to the fact that, while we had the same mother, Leah and I each had a different father than Charles, Stanley, and Cecil?

Our family's ethnicity sprang from a stock of Welsh, Irish, French, English, Jewish, Italian, Native American, and Black genes. Yet history, with the complicity of the academic world and the connivance of Jim Crow laws, has ignored the other components of our lineage and focused only on the Black, essentially by use of the blind and automatic categorization of the obvious misnomer "African American." We are not ashamed of our Black blood, but it is only *part* of who we are! Still, our family—most particularly me, with one parent of entirely Italian lineage and the other of mixed ancestry—was denied any recognition of the genes in our heritage other than Black.

Growing up in that "free" northern town, we never fit completely into commonly perceived characteristics of any one particular ethnic group. It was undoubtedly our familial experiences that shaped not just us but how we perceived the things that happened to us. Elkhart and the world labeled us "black," totally ignoring the other ethnicities that comprised our gene pool. We accepted that label and lived our lives accordingly, at least while young and living in

Elkhart, merely to survive. But still the world, in Charles Gordone's words, "chewed us up and spat us out."

This is one of the essential and pivotal points of this memoir, and one expounded for a lifetime by Gordone: that there cannot nor should there be any exclusivity or denial of the results obtained from such mixed blood. This is the very paradigm of the phrase "melting pot of America." Gordone also said, "You must find yourself in everybody, and not fall into the polarizing traps of color, class, religion, politics, etc."

In his play *No Place to Be Somebody,* Gordone was the first person I ever heard use the phrases "clean whites" and "dirty blacks." Had our parents put too much emphasis on trying to live as "clean whites," thereby alienating us from those *they* considered "dirty blacks" and who were such objects of scorn, derision, and disdain to them—although they kept those opinions well hidden from the outside world? Were we doomed to failure from the beginning in our dreams of finding a place to truly be somebody in an All-American America, when the world was only too quick to label us "colored" and therefore inferior?

We found out through experience, and despite our parents' caveats, that there are "dirty whites" and "clean blacks" as well. What made some of them that way? Had they too tried to live the American Dream only to fail, never finding a place where they could really be somebody? Or had they, like us, been fated to look in all the wrong places, at the wrong times, with the wrong people? By relating and revealing our problems, perhaps a discerning reader will be able to discover answers to the questions raised in this work.

The main body of this memoir has been divided according to the three major residence locations of our childhood, for the simple reason that these places contained the intrinsic dynamics that affected our futures. Vignettes under those headings relate some of our experiences at those particular times and places, as well as indicate our ages when these things happened.

For a deeper look into the psyche of Charles Gordone's childhood experiences and as an adjunct to this book you will want to read his soliloquy "Whiter Than Snow," Act Two, Scene 1, from his drama *No Place to Be Somebody*. The character of Gabe Gabriel defines and recounts some experiences I recognize as being familial. Since this role was closely patterned after Gordone's own life, it is tantamount to his own autobiography. You will readily see the deep impression events made on his young mind, and decipher easily those black-white-black relationships that existed both within the family circle and in the outside world. This soliloquy portrays life among the Gordons during childhood and growing up in Elkhart as nothing he later wrote could possibly do. These facts I know to be true for, like Charles, I too was there!

"Whiter Than Snow," taken from the old hymn of the same name, resonates with the scalding bitterness accrued by all of us—and Gordone in particular—as a result of living there, especially in our relations with the white world we were never totally accepted into and the black world so scathingly denounced in private by both our parents.

I also question what part was played by our intense involvement in a cult-type religion, one that was forced upon us by our mother. Remnants of those teachings and preachings appear throughout Gordone's play. Did her religious domination so penetrate our thinking that we were unable to assess its impact upon our minds and characters until much later in our lives? Did that religious observance as instilled by Mother give us higher aims and moral standards than we might otherwise have had?

What went into the mix that made one of us, out of five, become a Pulitzer Prize winner? Was it an inherited or a developed genius, or simply a melding of all his childhood experiences, both good and bad? Certainly we all had the same home life, religious upbringing, and educational opportunities. Each one of us, in varying degrees, also experienced the same things that happened to Charles.

The questions posed in this book often haunt me as I endeavor to find the answers. There is no single incident I can point to and say, "There, *that* is what made Gordone the man he became!"

This book is composed of childhood memories, often expressed in childish words, for I have attempted to recount these events just as they happened when I was a child. Of necessity I have had to include not just my own but the stories of some of those who also touched our lives. I lay no claim to infallibility; therefore it is quite possible that what seemed to me to be "thus and so" was not seen in the same way or context by others. These are, however, *my* personal recollections of things past.

So, with a lot of help from Charles, I am inviting you to come, take memory's journey with me. Despite many bumps in the road, a few detours, and even some bad weather along the way, at the very least we will have a trip!

Camille Gordon, 1965, about sixty-one years of age.
Courtesy of Alexander Tschumakow.

1

Mother

OUR MOTHER, CAMILLE, was a beautiful woman. She was Creole-like in appearance—tall, fair-skinned, with a golden dust of freckles across her nose, a cloud of dark hair, and luminous eyes. Those high cheekbones, inherited from her part–Native American mother and passed on to all her children, shaped a face and forehead that indicated high intelligence. She was indeed a woman with a brilliant mind, yet seemingly she never used it to its fullest capability. Vivacious in her personality and aptly described as a cross between Lena Horne and Minnie Pearl, Camille possessed a memory that amazed everyone with whom she came in contact. She was definitely someone to be reckoned with.

Born Novis Camille Morgan to Edward Lee and Nora Gilbert Morgan on November 6, 1904, in Martin, Tennessee, she was the third of five children. Her younger years were spent in Tennessee and then Kentucky.

Mother always bewailed the fact that she felt unloved and starved for affection, expressing and reiterating that desire over the entire eighty-nine years of her life—indeed, up to the very day she passed away, on November 9, 1993.

She acknowledged there were lots of people who said they loved her, but something inside never let her fully believe their avowals. There was an inner need going deeper into her psyche than mere words, yet none of us could ever figure out exactly what it was she craved.

Apparently even Daddy couldn't satisfy whatever her deep-seated yearning was. He was not a demonstrative man, not given to the affectionate word or the quick hug or kiss. He believed that men not only didn't cry but also never exhibited their emotions, and that actions spoke louder than words. He was a man unable to verbalize his feelings.

I'm sure he thought that providing in every possible way for the family (even though four of us children were not even his own!) was more than sufficient proof of his love. It never seemed enough to satisfy Mother. Once, I asked if she thought Daddy loved her, and her enigmatic response was, "Well, I guess he does . . . as much as he's capable of loving *anyone*." What a burden for a man to carry for the sixty-four years of marriage they shared!

Neither of her parents could give her the assurance she needed, for they were just as uncommunicative and undemonstrative as Daddy was. The only one of Mother's siblings who seemed able to elicit love from Grandmother was her "baby," Aunt Lula, upon whom love and attention were lavished. Only fourteen when her first child was born, Grandmother had a lot of growing up of her own to do, while Grandpa was just as reticent in showing affection as was Daddy. This made for as much sibling rivalry for love and attention among the Morgan children as it did the Gordons. Otherwise, it appears that only with their grandchildren were either set of grandparents able to express love, whether in word or by deed.

A possible explanation for Mother's desperately seeking love may have been a traumatic event that occurred when she was about two years old. There was a man, a so-called family friend, who frequently visited the Morgan home in the South. Always, the first thing he wanted to do was hold Mother on his lap. What no adult seemed to be aware of was that underneath her little dress he was doing unpleasant things with his finger. She would cry out to her parents, especially to her mother, crying, squirming, and twisting in an effort to get down. Grandmother would push her back in place and scold her, "Oh, he's a *nice* man, he's our friend, and see, he *likes* you!" She never questioned the reason for Mother's obvious discomfort, perhaps shrugging it off as a certain timidity some children exhibit around strangers. Mother never told me how many occurrences of this kind there were, but intimated they had been numerous.

Back in those days, child abuse—whether mental, physical, or sexual—was a subject neither recognized nor acknowledged, and certainly not ever verbally discussed. Studies over the past few years indicate this type of molestation frequently was committed by family members, by relatives, and even more often by close friends, all people upon whom the shroud of suspicion seldom, if ever, fell. What could a mere child do when these acts were performed? What words could a two-year-old articulate that would explain her discomfort? All Mother knew was that it was painful. Appeals for help from the parents who were supposed to care for, love, and protect her fell on deaf ears.

Too young to express what was going on, she eventually concluded that they must not really love her since they neither investigated nor rescued her from this maltreatment. Thus, the conviction that expressed love wasn't necessarily true became deeply embedded in Mother's young mind, and it haunted her for a lifetime.

Another shocking experience in her young life, one that bore also the bitter fruit of questionable guilt, was the death of her baby sister, Rosa Eline, which happened when the baby was only five months old and Mother was just fourteen. Grandmother had stayed up nursing the sick infant for several days and nights until she became so exhausted she simply had to get some rest. Grandmother lay down on her bed, telling Mother to stay awake and keep close watch over the baby, calling her if the need arose. Mother must have dozed off at times during the night, for when she and Grandmother woke up the next morning Rosa had died.

"You've killed my baby! You've killed your baby sister! If you had stayed awake, my baby wouldn't have died!" Grandmother was inconsolable, but how does a teenager reply to such accusations, and how had she continued living her life with a mother who had called her a murderer?

From the symptoms Mother described when telling of this tragedy, we felt the baby must have died of pneumonia, which was a death sentence in those days, for penicillin and antibiotics were not yet in common use. Even today, pneumonia claims far too many lives.

Grandmother held that baby's death against Mother for a long, long time. And Mother was always unsure if the accusations held any truth or not. If Grandmother had been watching, would the baby have lived? Or died anyway? If Mother hadn't dozed off, what effect would there have been? At any rate, the end result was inescapable: the baby died.

For the rest of her life Mother solicited love from her parents, most particularly from her mother, always seeking some sign of forgiveness, of caring; but she was never completely satisfied with the ways in which they exhibited their feelings. These may also be among the reasons that Mother never once verbally expressed to her own children that we were loved—which, in turn, made us work like little beavers for at least some indication of affection or approval. We felt that if we "grew up to be somebody," or made her proud of us, she wouldn't be able to *not* love us. Just to say to us, "I love you," was a simple enough phrase, but it never once crossed her lips. Did she feel her actions in cooking, cleaning, and looking after us were evidence enough? If so, she was as uncommunicative as her parents and Daddy.

Another example of Grandmother's "deaf ear" took place on a warm summer day. School was out for the summer and all the children in the neighborhood were enjoying their liberty. A recent electrical storm had knocked down an old oak tree not far from the Morgan residence. All the kids living nearby were having fun jumping up and down on the springy branches. Mother asked Grandmother's permission to also go and play but was told, "No way!"

Mother sneaked off anyway and was having a good old time until she slipped and fell, with the pointed end of one of the branches penetrating her leg. Unaware of her mishap, the others continued jumping up and down while the embedded branch dug even more deeply into her leg. Once they finally realized what had happened, they lifted Mother up and carried her home, bleeding profusely and crying with pain. They deposited her into Grandmother's hands.

Immediately, Grandmother ranted at her, "Don't 'spect me to do nothin' fer you. This is what you git for not mindin' me, so you kin jus' sit back and take yore punishment!" Mother had to clean and bandage the wound herself. She received two scars from that experience: one on her leg, the other on her soul.

These may have also been among the subconscious reasons that Mother never spoke up for either Stanley or Leah when Daddy physically abused them. And she wielded a mean belt herself on occasion; she had been unable to stop beating me, as related in the chapter "The Bicycle," when she was in a fit of anger. She turned a deaf ear to our cries because no one had rescued *her* when she was being abused or wrongly accused. She was only doing what had been done to her by the adults who peopled her world: nothing.

It is a sad but true fact—one that child psychologists increasingly stress—that most parents do to their children what has been done to them. Without help and guidance, they repeat their own and their parents' mistakes over and over again, unless and until they gain the strength and knowledge to change their behavior patterns.

It is also true that simply witnessing the abuse of a family member (whether the abuse is physical or mental) can cause a permanent and deep-seated scarring of children's psyches, even if they are not the ones feeling the pain of punishment.

Our childhood was a living example of the "witness" effect, especially for Charles and myself, since it always seemed to be Leah or Stanley being punished. Charles and I evidently were better at recalling what we were *not* supposed to do, but we too were deeply marked by what we saw.

Grandmother's deaf ear repeated itself in the deaf ear of Mother when her own children uttered cries of pain. My own "deaf ear" took the form of losing my hearing, in a subconscious and symbolic revolt against the extreme verbal and physical harshness that permeated our daily lives. Not to "hear" something enabled me to deny its reality, and if it wasn't real, it could not possibly exist.

As a little girl, I thought there was no one like my mother, and I hung around her like a bee does around honey. We went everywhere together, and to make her proud of me and thereby love me unconditionally, I did exactly as she told me, to the extent that it was possible. To arouse her displeasure or anger raised the dire specter of the five of us being put into an oft-threatened orphanage. It behooved all of us to toe the line she had drawn for us.

Seemingly, this was seldom a problem for Charles or me; it was usually Stanley or Leah who provoked those extreme outbursts of venomous punishment from Daddy, most often when we were seated together at the dinner table. There never seemed to be anything we could do to forestall any such actions, and during these abusive punishments Mother never said a word, nor did she even have so much as a tear in her eye.

Doing exactly what she and Daddy wanted assured us of their love forever—we thought! Little did any of us understand we were yearning and searching for that unconditional love that is every child's birthright. This quest ended only after we became young adults and left home, hoping to find someone out there who would give us the unconditional love we sought. Stanley, Leah, and Cecil, our siblings, had given up in early childhood the hope of ever being able to please our parents, so as they grew up they could scarcely wait to be on their own.

Just entering her teens when the Morgans moved to Elkhart, Mother was immediately enrolled in the old Ward Block Schools 4 and 5, later known as Lincoln, and then went on to Roosevelt Junior High, where she was an excellent scholar and sports figure—both genes that Charles definitely inherited (and, to a lesser extent, our other brothers also). Grandmother kept a framed photo on her bedroom wall of Mother seated in the front middle row of the girls' volleyball team at Roosevelt, where she was the captain. I recently found that old sepia photo, one that had always amused Mother because it was difficult to pick her out from the group of white girls.

Skin color was always something that mattered to her. She was never happier than when someone mistook her for "white." Yet color was something Charles and I were continually faced with, especially when some white person apparently couldn't tell what ethnicity we were just by looking at us, or from our hair, or from the way we talked and acted. They seemed to dislike *us* if anyone quite casually remarked, "Oh yes, the Gordons, they are a very nice colored family." It seemed they felt we had in some way tried to fool them into thinking we were something other than what we appeared to be.

The truth was, Charles and I didn't think in terms of color, only in terms of people's abilities. Those same people wanted to categorize, pigeonhole, and stereotype us and force us into the mental slots formed by their own learned prejudices as to what they thought colored people really were: lazy, buffoons, unintelligent, incapable of accomplishing even the most basic standard of living a white person might have. We were never, ever supposed to endeavor to rise to (or above) certain stations in life that were considered the norm for whites, but unthinkable for colored people to aspire to.

Since we defied and challenged their narrow-minded concepts, however innocently, they were unable to accept us. They were angered by what they perceived as an attempt on our part to be just like them, and desirous instead of clinging to their own myths of colored people as an inferior race. Even though Mother and Daddy expressed some of those same prejudices in the privacy of their own home, Charles and I truly believed (if we thought about it at all) that we were the same as anyone—regardless of race, creed, or color—most specifically because of our *abilities.*

In 1930 Charles started kindergarten at Lincoln Elementary School, primarily because the church school he later attended for a short time didn't have that grade. Charles never forgot the occasion when the teacher decided to put on a play and selected *Little Black Sambo.* A little white boy wanted to be the tiger, while the teacher wanted Charles to play Sambo—but she hadn't thought of Mother's possible reaction to this endeavor. Suffice it to say that when Mother found out about it, she let the teacher know in no uncertain terms that *her* little boy was not going to play *anybody's* little black Sambo! The teacher then talked the other little boy's mother into letting him play the lead role, and cast Charles instead as the tiger. But when the other boy found he would be required to wear black grease paint he rebelled, so his mom fixed up a black stocking to fit over his head, with holes cut out for the eyes and mouth.

During the performance the tiger is supposed to put on Sambo's clothes, but struggle as he might, Charles couldn't get them on. "Sambo" tried to help him, taking off his black stocking mask in order to do so. This sight tickled the audience so much they roared with laughter, which the other little boy swore ended his acting career—but it served to whet Charles's appetite for being on stage. Charles pointed out, "Hey, I didn't have to be white to play the tiger, and that boy could wear a costume to make him *any* color!"

This little vignette also serves to point out the following factors: (1) there were some racial tensions back in 1930; (2) teachers were beginning to try to get parents involved at school; and (3) kids bore the brunt of it all.

This was one of Charles's first initiations into the "white mask, black world" syndrome. You could present a "white" face (or mask) in your actions and words to the public, but if you were colored, you were irretrievably cast into the black world. We didn't know it at the time, but it would become a lifelong obsession for Gordone to try and destroy "masks" wherever they might crop up, to dig below the surface and slash through superficialities to discover a person's *real* identity, the one hidden behind the mask. It was all part of his later dreams of inclusion in the American theater.

When Mother finished school in Elkhart, including graduating from Elkhart Business University, she moved to Cleveland, Ohio, where she worked as a stenographer before she married one Charles J. Fleming. Charles Edward was born eleven months later. Immediately she became pregnant again with Stanley, but by the time Cecil was born in 1928 the marriage was definitely over and she had returned to her parents' home with her three sons.

With Grandmother taking care of the boys, Mother rejoined the work force as an elevator operator at the Hotel Elkhart. Sometimes she took Charles with her, letting him ride on the elevator or play with a little white boy whose father operated the cigar counter in the hotel lobby. Charles couldn't have been more than three years old, an outgoing and gregarious child. That little boy, whose name was Ted Strouse, later became a friend and classmate of Charles; both of them were members of the graduating Elkhart High School class of 1944. In later years, Ted wrote me a note to indicate he and his father had never forgotten those days of elevator riding—or of simply playing in the hotel lobby with the little boy who grew up to become a Pulitzer Prize winner.

Shortly after that, while Mother was working for one Stephen Anthony D'Antini as his housekeeper, their relationship escalated and Mother became pregnant with me. I didn't discover my true parentage until I was about fifteen years old, and the knowledge came to me quite accidentally. While cleaning house for Mother one summer day, I recalled a rolled-up paper in the top of her and Daddy's chest of drawers. As something that we had never been allowed to examine, it quite naturally held some fascination for us, especially me. On this particular day Mother was at work, with Leah and I delegated to cleaning house. I'll never know what motivated me that day, but curiosity overcame me. I marched into their bedroom and removed the scroll from the drawer.

To my great chagrin and surprise, it was a marriage certificate for Mother and Daddy, but the date on it was almost a full two years *after* my birthdate of December 30, 1929. I couldn't believe my eyes. Showing the paper to Leah, I said sarcastically, "Well, she must have been pregnant before she and Daddy got married, so I must be illegitimate, and if that's true, how can she expect *me* to be someone when *she* wasn't?"

Leah made no comment one way or another at that time, but a few days later, provoked at me about something, she not only told Mother what I had done but also recounted my scathing remarks afterward. There was no reaction or explanation from Mother.

A few days later, a Sunday, as usual I was in the basement helping Mother do the family laundry. She and I had spent a few uneasy days avoiding each other's glances. I couldn't look her in the eye, and she seemed to be having trouble looking into mine. Then, in an apologetic tone of voice that I'd never before heard from her, she explained the circumstances of my birth.

The facts as she related them were these: my father, who was from Sicily, was twenty years older than my mother, but he had loved her very much and pleaded with her to marry him. From what she said, he was an affectionate and loving person, quite often stroking her hair and telling her how much he loved her. Upset at her refusal to marry him, he left his job with the railroad and moved to another town in Indiana—I believe it was called Silver Creek. If he ever returned to Elkhart, perhaps to visit relatives, Mother never knew about it. Putting love aside, Mother said she wouldn't marry him because Grandmother swore she would "rather see her in her grave than married to a white man." (Talk about reverse discrimination!)

It was many years later before Mother's two sisters, Lula and Bea, talked about this to me. Both told me how much he had loved my mother and that if he had known of her pregnancy he would never have accepted her rejection of his marriage proposal. But after that first discussion, Mother seldom made reference to the events surrounding my birth, at least insofar as they related to his being my "real" father.

With four children all born within a five-year period, this was undoubtedly why she married William Gordon, for he promised to help her raise us. Ironically, Grandmother hadn't wanted her to marry Bill Gordon, either, because of his dark complexion, but I'm sure the economic pressures of the Depression played a large role in her acceptance.

For my part, I felt that Bill Gordon was the only father I had ever known; he had cared for and provided for me, and his love for me was never in question. Mother did say that Daddy had asked her if my father was "one of the niggers here in Elkhart," and she could truthfully say no. It never occurred to him, nor did he ever know, that my father was white, let alone Italian, and it never seemed of any importance to him that I was fair-skinned—or, as colored folks put it, "looked like white." I sincerely believe it was my loving obedience to him, as opposed to the more angry responses of my siblings, that totally gained his love. Certainly my feelings for him never changed; for the rest of our lives, to me he was always "Daddy."

After their marriage and when I was three, Mother and Daddy produced a daughter, my sister Leah. Mother told me she had thought she was "through having children" after I was born, but since Daddy had never had a child of his own blood, she felt he deserved one. They decided to raise the two of us as "sisters," with the boys knowing their father was Charles Fleming. We all went by the name of Gordon during childhood, and it was only later that Stanley and Cecil opted to go by the Fleming name when they entered the armed services. Charles kept the name of Gordon until years later, when he made minor alterations in it for stage purposes.

I don't know why Mother became interested in the Seventh-day Adventist Church, which she joined when I was about two and a half years old and Charles was about five and a half, but as we grew older we couldn't understand why everything about it had to be so harsh, unyielding, and dreary. Brought up in the African Methodist Episcopal Church, she had become Catholic to please her first husband. All four of us had been christened in the Catholic Church.

I believe she had some obscure desire that made her need to suffer. At first, Daddy was a bit intrigued by this "new" religion, but he shortly lost any interest, and in fact became quite acrimonious about it. His objections to her religious observances led to many heated arguments between them, to the point of violence on one occasion. I believe she felt going to a priest to confess and then receiving absolution for her "sins" was too easy an out; she had to *suffer.*

Mother seemed obsessed by the teaching that we are all sinners, and she clasped that belief tightly to her bosom. I don't know exactly what she felt she had done in her life that made her think she could only hope to be "saved" from sin by the Second Coming of Christ. She professed a strong belief in God's promises; through my own experiences I found that whatever one does, God cannot be bargained with, and you cannot demand that He "deliver the goods" on His promises according to what *you* want. I never understood how she could adamantly insist that we not be *of* or *in* the world, staying separate and apart, yet expend all her efforts in insisting we gain the world's approval and recognition. What a strange and devious dichotomy, to be sure, one that was nearly impossible for us to reconcile with the demands she made upon us.

"Be sure your sins will find you out" was one of her most frequent admonishments, but to me the most frightening teaching of all was "The wages of sin are death." It was never clear to me how one could repent of sin, ask for and receive forgiveness, and turn away from that sin—yet be told that you would still have to pay for having done so in the first place.

It was graphically impressed on our young minds that while one may be physically burnt in this life here on earth, at some point one loses consciousness and no longer feels pain. We were told that sinners, on the contrary, would be cast into the inferno of a lake of fire and would never be beyond feeling that pain. They would feel it all through their bodies until their very last cells had been consumed. This was what was termed "burning in hell for eternity."

Quite frankly, it scared the pants off all five of us kids! No wonder one of my most horrible nightmares featured me in a "lake of fire," being roasted on a spit like a pig while devilish imps jumped around, laughing with glee at my pleas for help. I concluded the most logical way to avoid such suffering would be to never sin at all, *not ever.* But then we were told that we are all sinners! What a Catch-22.

The little colored congregation Mother started (in a little building her sister Bea had purchased) furnished an ideal stage for her love of the spotlight; she inculcated that same love in Charles and myself. She dreamed and planned for the day Charles would become a preacher, but he had dreams of his own. He was interested instead in music, acting, and writing, all of which involved him being "center stage" and ultimately led to his move to California after his stint in the armed services. Mother then turned her eyes on me, but after my hearing loss killed her visions of me as a concert pianist, she decided to groom me into her ideal of a preacher's wife.

Elkhart was not far from our denomination's college in Berrien Springs, Michigan, and Mother arranged with the college to have ministerial students come to our small church so they could practice preaching. All the young male students were invited to our home for dinner after morning services. It seemed the Gordon home was the only one that offered them any hospitality; I think Mother was checking them out as potential husbands for me! Strangely, though, she flirted with them as if she were interested in them for herself. They couldn't have seen much of me because Mother hogged the limelight, entirely dominating the conversation. Poor Daddy scarcely got a word in edgewise and seemed relieved when it was time to return to work. Mother was truly a premier cook, however, and once these young men tasted her food they never refused an invitation.

Regardless of Mother's belief in her religion, I thought it a terrible thing to harass our grandparents into joining that church in their eighties. She threatened not to take care of them in their old age if they didn't join; this reminded me too much of her threats to put all of her children in an orphanage if she wasn't strictly obeyed or didn't get what she wanted.

During our childhood, Mother would never talk about the boys' father despite their many inquiries, and I only recently found out he had been born in Connorsville, Indiana, the son of Robert and Mary Robeson Fleming. We have often speculated upon how the two of them ended up together in Cleveland, Ohio, he to father three sons with her, and yet she would never answer any of Charles's questions about him: What kind of work did he do? What sort of person was he? Did he still live? Were there perhaps other relatives still living?

A copy of their marriage license indicates he was a clerk, she a stenographer, and was issued in the name "Canville Morgan." (I assume this was a typographical error and should have read, "Camille.") I note also that on Charles's birth certificate his parents' residence was given as 7509 Woodland Avenue, Suite #4. Was this a hotel? Offices? Or perhaps an apartment building?

Years later I went online and discovered that Mr. Fleming had later resided in northern California, had been a mortician, and according to his obituary was a devoted family man. Were there children born of that second union? Could there be half-sisters or brothers living in the Sonoma area where his father and stepmother lived? Charles had wanted so desperately to know more about him.

Charles mentioned that one of his earliest memories, although hazy, was of an older couple who took care of him, seemingly in Cleveland. The gentleman wore a fez and smoked a hookah pipe. He often wondered if they could have been his paternal grandparents. Mother would neither corroborate nor deny that vague memory, refusing to tell him anything. Even in the last few years of her life she would not speak to any of the boys about their father.

I do know Charles pursued a trail to Chicago, and another time to Oakland, California, on a quest in his later life, but he was never able to obtain any answers to his questions. And on one of Mother's trips to California to visit our brother Stanley in Berkeley (where her brother Algie and his family also lived), someone—perhaps her sister-in-law—took her someplace in the Oakland area to see one Charles Fleming, but she would never answer any questions as to whether or not it was the boys' father she had located. Stone wall!

Sometime in her twenties Mother developed the art of public speaking, which she seemed to have been born into. As what was commonly called in those days an *elocutionist*, she displayed an amazing talent for the memorization and recitation of vast quantities of works by such writers and poets as W. E. B. DuBois, Langston Hughes, and James Weldon Johnson. Those were among the good days of our childhood, for Mother practiced on all five of us. These writers' words were fed to us on a daily basis as our entrée, with generous servings of Paul Laurence Dunbar for dessert!

I can never forget her recitation of Dunbar's "Little Brown Baby Wif' De Spahklin' Eyes" to baby Leah, who gurgled and smiled, all the time listening intently, happy to be the center of attention. We all hung on every word Mother spoke. At our most impressionable ages, those lofty ideals were indelibly etched upon our young minds, and we all—especially the young Charles—soon adopted their thoughts as our very own. The fires of ambition and aspiration were kindled in his heart, and they burned for his entire life.

Mother became quite in demand as an entertainer by reciting both prose and poetry before various groups around the city—some colored, many white. She performed before all the white service and social clubs: Moose, Eagles, Elks, Italian-American Club, Lions and Kiwanis, the Sunday Evening Club, and others. She was always paid, enabling her to earn a bit of spending change as well as bask in the limelight she so dearly loved. After I began playing the piano, she added a musical background to several of her recitations, which was also enjoyed by her audiences.

Some of these readings were quite lengthy, for example, "The Party" by Dunbar, which takes up more than seven pages in his book *Lyrics of Lowly Life.* A dentist from Chicago, Dr. Andrew J. Dobson, had written a book titled *Uncle Joe's Journal,* and his writings and poetry also became part of her presentations. Dr. Dobson's stated aim was "to make the white man laugh and, while he had his mouth open, give him a little dose of castor oil!" This aim was also evidenced in many of Mother's readings, with the possible exception of the entertaining and humorous ones; they were intended to make white people stop and think about their treatment and stereotypical views of colored folks. Perfectly at ease on the stage, she never forgot a word, and since much of the prose did not rhyme, I sensed I was in the presence of someone with a tremendous capacity for memorization.

When and where did she find time to learn all this material? One would think that caring for five children and a husband would have taken up every moment she had. But it was truly a treasure and an inspiration for us, because such early exposure to all those lofty ideals meant they were never to be forgotten. They served as a bellwether in our search for higher things in life. This turned out to be the most important thing she ever did for us as we searched for meaning and substance in our own lives.

During Charles's New York years and my life in California, contact between siblings lay in the fact that we called Mother long-distance nearly every Sunday for years. (Charles also made numerous trips to my home in Altadena, California, whenever business brought him to the West Coast. He also made periodic visits to Elkhart.) Mother, in turn, passed on the news from all of her children, one to the other, so we were constantly aware of what each sibling was doing. She enjoyed being the mother of a Pulitzer Prize winner, for that reflected glory on both her and Daddy and made her proud of Charles. Still, Charles couldn't understand why she never took the time to read either his play or his other writings. He often reflected that she had never seemed to see him for who he really was.

After we had all left home and were involved in our own lives, and after the passing of our grandparents, it was as though something was released in her that made her determined, finally, to show people that *she* had value and worth, totally separate and aside from her unfulfilled dreams for her offspring. She and Daddy had rejoined the white First Seventh-day Adventist Church, the reason being that—according to both of them—"niggers are too hard to get along with."

This step was taken only after she had joined the colored churches of South Bend, Indiana, and Cassopolis, Michigan, both of which repudiated her efforts and demands to be their "leader," a star, the only one who knew how things should be accomplished in the congregation. They refused to look upon her as she wanted to be considered, for in both those churches there were those who could see through her machinations, who refused to look upon her as a prophet sent by God. Unable to manipulate those members, in a huff she quit, still seeking a place where *she* could be the big "somebody," taking Daddy with her.

The white church suited them just fine because the congregation accepted her at face value, while she didn't have to worry about a deep social or personal relationship with any members who didn't want to be close friends. A number of them did welcome invitations to dinner, for she was indeed a premier cook.

There were so many things we wanted to know the truth about that she would never relate to us, and we had to delve into them on our own, making errors of judgment and understanding until we were finally brought up short, face to face with things she could have enlightened us about but refused to do so. I trust you can sense some of the ways she wielded a terrible influence over us, yet on occasion some good also was accomplished. If you find any similarity to errors in your own life, I urge you to take steps *now* to obtain the help and guidance that will enable you to change and correct your mistakes instead of repeating them. By doing this you can break the cycle of hurt and bitterness that no child should know. Every child is indeed entitled to unconditional love, and it is unquestionably every child's birthright.

2

Daddy

BORN IN PARIS, TENNESSEE, on March 15, 1897, Daddy often spoke of how his mother passed away when he was eight years old. I believe he felt his life might have been different with a mother's gentling influence; instead, he had a cruel father who delighted in punishing him for the least infraction and became Daddy's reason for leaving home in his early teens. Young though he was, he had already gained a reputation among the adults in that small Tennessee town for being truthful, straightforward, and fair, which seemed to follow wherever he went. He knew the value of even a penny, let alone a dime, and his motto was "waste not, want not." He was also a morally clean man, and I don't believe that in all the years he and Mother were married did he so much as look at another woman.

Daddy had been married once before, briefly, to an older woman who died; her daughter Aletha was not only Mother's age, but also

Mother's best friend and schoolmate. Daddy never mentioned that Aletha is named in Elkhart history books as the first colored graduate of Elkhart High School, class of 1925. I suppose that would have been tantamount to admitting there were some colored people in Elkhart who also wanted to amount to something and who had accomplished something.

Now, Daddy had some strange ideas about colored people. While brown-skinned himself, he didn't like his own race and didn't want to live around them, although he had done so when he had first moved to Elkhart. He often said the average colored person living in Elkhart wasn't trying to *do* anything or *be* somebody, and the only way "they" could carry you was DOWN. It was years later before I discovered that a lady we all knew, Rose H. Mathews, had been active in Girl Reserves, the Glee Club, in plays, and the French Club—albeit in segregated facilities for the Girl Reserves. She was a member of the class of 1932. Also, the first colored athlete at Elkhart High School, Barney Phillips, class of 1934, sang in the Glee Club, played a part in a school musical, *The Minstrel,* in 1933, and won honors for the school as a member of the mile relay team in track. This information was never imparted to us, and I was quite surprised, because we all knew Barney, his wife, and his entire family. If Daddy didn't know all this, I'm sure Mother did.

I recently read *The River Flows Backward* by one Ben Barnes, of Elkhart, and while there were parts that indicated Mr. Barnes's father tried to inspire his sons to be "men," my thoughts after reading and rereading the book were, "Now I understand why Daddy didn't want to raise us kids over on the South Side, especially my sister and me!" It seemed all the boys were interested in was making out with the girls. But the book did indicate that there were some colored people in Elkhart who wanted to do something or be somebody; Daddy and Mother certainly did not have a corner on *that* market!

Anything good that had ever been done for Daddy, he swore, had been done by white folks, never colored people. He told us how, in his younger days, a white man he'd once worked for cautioned him, "Bill, don't ever marry a black, *black* woman, because they are evil, mean-tempered, and hard to get along with." A lot of colored people also bought into that belief. Daddy admitted one of the main reasons he wanted to marry Mother was that he figured she was as close to white as he'd ever be able to get. Acting and thinking like "white" may have been his life's goal, but it certainly couldn't change the color of his skin.

Daddy also told me, in later years, that when he looked in the mirror while shaving he incredulously asked God, "Why and how in the world did You make something so *black* and *ugly?*" I never thought of him as being ugly; to me he looked the way he looked, and that was that. And he certainly wasn't the darkest-colored person we ever saw! Still, it was difficult to conceal my feelings of revulsion when I heard either or both of them refer to another colored person as *darky* or *nigger,* which seemed a permanent part of their vocabulary.

The concept of light skin versus dark among colored folk themselves was always a puzzle to me. With a rainbow of colors right in our own family, how could one be "better" than another? We were sternly admonished and strictly taught that color was only the outside show: it was what you were inside, in your head and your heart, that was important. Charles and I took that precept to our hearts, choosing to follow what we were told and not what was exemplified in front of us. Skin color has never mattered to either him or me.

I have wondered many times about apparent discrepancies in the average colored person's attitudes and beliefs about color differences within our race itself, so it was no surprise to me when in later years I came across the results of a study by Charles H. Parrish that had appeared in the *Journal of Negro Education* in 1946.[1] I realize that his conclusions were obtained in the mid-1940s, but this made them all the more applicable to people of my parents' age group. His study may partially explain the beliefs of people who lived in the time span between 1920 and 1950. Few people will admit to those feelings, but the fact remains that some of us suffered from those stereotypical views! Being called "high yaller," "honky," or "spook" by one's own race is a degrading experience that happened more often than folks are willing to admit or talk about! I also wonder, if this study were made today, how the results would compare.

Mr. Parrish's conclusions about the people he interviewed were given in percentages as follows:

	Light Negroes	*Medium Brown Negroes*	*Dark Negroes*	*All or No Answer*
Hard to get along with	23.2	9.9	52.5	14.1
Think they are better	74.7	9.4	2.9	13.0
Sweet and affectionate	15.5	57.7	7.9	18.9
Sensitive about color	16.8	4.6	68.4	10.2
Aggressive about rights	31.9	28.4	22.8	16.9
Physically stronger	6.5	12.1	59.4	22.0
Teacher's favorites	62.6	19.6	5.0	12.8
Excluded from sororities	0.23	8.7	75.0	16.1

Before proposing to Mother, Daddy was determined to find out if she could cook, so he invited himself to Sunday dinner and offered to provide the meat, a pot roast; it was so delicious, he asked Mother right on the spot to marry him. Mother may have married him in order to have help raising four young children, but the way to *his* heart was definitely through his stomach. I believe he may have gotten the best end of that bargain; children grow up and leave the nest, but a wife usually will care for you for all of your days. While Daddy might have quibbled over buying toilet paper, he never hesitated to purchase whatever she needed to cook with, especially when Depression days began to fade. His only requisite: whatever was cooked had to be eaten. Totally. There was no such thing as a "leftover" in our house.

Many people can testify to Mother's cooking prowess. Of Grandmother's three daughters, she was the best cook, a fact readily admitted even by the other two. We were vegetarians in accordance with Mother's religious beliefs. Daddy was satisfied to go along with this because vegetables for seven were certainly cheaper than meat. We had turkey only for Thanksgiving and Christmas, with fried chicken once or twice in the summer, but that was the sum total of our meat-eating. Pork was definitely never in our house because it was considered unclean.

Once in a while a family friend would drop off a "mess" of freshly caught fish, which Mother would cook, providing they were biblically acceptable (they had to have both fins and scales). There was scarcely a bone left when we finished, either. During World War II meat was rationed, so Mother gave our meat coupons to our grandparents—which bothered us not at all, for we couldn't miss something we'd never had.

We were lucky enough to live near a farming community, so vegetables and fruits were plentiful, varied, and relatively cheap. We also ate a lot of dried beans, my favorite being navy beans. I was much chagrined to find in later years the reason we had so many of the latter was that owing to the Depression, money was scarce. I had been positive it was because they knew how I loved those beans! Secretly I always yearned to occasionally put a little catsup in them, but Daddy considered that a "condiment" and not something that was good or necessary for us. We didn't even have catsup in the house. I noticed, however, he had no problem with Mother's pickled pears, or her sweet pickles and such, not to mention all the homemade jellies and jams. That was different; those were things *he* liked!

Like any self-respecting housewife of her day, Mother did a lot of canning of foods for the winter, and Daddy seemed to buy everything that could be put up in a jar. I've often wondered how they determined how many jars were needed, for we never ran out from winter to summer. Canning was a family project, and since we would all be sharing this bounty, Daddy insisted we kids help in whatever way Mother needed us. This usually meant we helped get the produce ready to be "put up." The entire family got up in the summer at 4:00 a.m., even though it was still dark, to go to a town called Bristol, Indiana, about nine miles away, where the "fruit hills" were located. Bristol had a small population, but the surrounding area was composed almost entirely of farms. There were acres and acres of rolling farmland planted with all kinds of fruits, berries, and vegetables, much cheaper if you chose to pick them yourselves—which Daddy did. Other people might buy theirs already picked, but not the Gordons! So, pick them we did: bushels of peaches, pears, apples, and plums; dozens upon dozens of ears of corn; mountains of green beans; tons of tomatoes. In season, there were crates of cherries, huckleberries, and strawberries; the crates were considered a good thing because the boys could use them to make their wagons and scooters. Mother also made all kinds of fruit preserves, jellies, and jams, while our own grape arbor provided the fruit for making grape juice. Nothing bought in a store ever equaled the taste of those home-canned foodstuffs.

From the basement's cold cellar, Daddy brought up bushel baskets of empty quart jars, which by his instructions and insistence had been assiduously saved and stored from the previous winter's use. It was Mother's responsibility to inspect these for any chipping, then wash and sterilize them while the five of us peeled, pared, pitted, and sliced; the only things we might have to purchase were a few new jars to replace any damaged ones, rubber seals, and Mason jar lids, plus a small amount of paraffin for jellies (we also washed off and saved the paraffin from any items as they were used). And believe me, Daddy supervised our K.P.! Parings and peelings had to be made to the correct depth, not too thick, or you'd get a stern lecture on waste. He always made sure there were enough paring knives for all of us, but after a few days, one of the boys (usually Charles, because he couldn't bear not being able to run and jump) would, "by mistake," throw a knife out with the peelings and we'd be one short. DIDN'T WORK. Daddy would simply stop and buy a couple more. He felt it was only fair that we all share in this work. And Daddy, after all the preparations for picking everything, still went to put in a full day's work at the YWCA after getting us started on the day's "program."

There were certain rules our parents had, in concert, spelled out for us in our tender, early years, the first being total, absolute obedience. We were not allowed to make decisions for ourselves; nor did they seek out our opinions on anything. They were firm believers that a child should be seen and not heard. We were told when to get up, what to wear, what to think, what to do, how to act, and where we could go. We didn't much care for this strict regime; the boys followed it out of fear of Daddy, but for me it was simply the way things were. I knew no other.

Sensing increasing undercurrents of tension in Mother and Daddy's relationship, we were all a bit uneasy. None of us wanted to be the cause of a "blow-up" between them. After all, if anything caused them to get a divorce, where would that leave us?

We could hear their voices coming upstairs through the air register after we were in bed, and it seemed they were always arguing about something. Long after Leah and my brothers were asleep, I could hear them still, their raised voices issuing either from below or from behind their closed bedroom door. I couldn't understand what they were saying, only the tone of their voices, but it seemed as though Daddy was always browbeating Mother about one thing or another. It was small wonder that every evening after supper, she "rested" on the studio couch at one end of the dining room, usually falling asleep and turning a deaf ear to any and all noises the rest of the family might make. Finally, upstairs in my bed, I pulled the covers over my head to keep from hearing their voices, in order to get any sleep at all.

Our first duty was to obey Daddy, as his word was law, even for Mother—which to us meant they shared a common God-head: disobey, and you faced the promise, the threat, of punishment, of abandonment, of eternal hellfire and damnation. I never heard Mother remonstrate with him over any discipline or abuse he chose to exercise, whether verbal or physical, and there was plenty of both in our young lives. If ever she disagreed with him, it was never evidenced in front of us. "Honor thy father and thy mother" wasn't just something we read in the Bible; it was literally drummed into us every day of our lives.

Early on we became a bit confused about the separation of God, Daddy, and Mother, and just which was which, or was to be most feared. We settled on our parents first, which could be either Daddy or Mother depending on who was raising the most hell that day; God came next, after them, for they were always present, while we couldn't see or hear God! If one of us was doing something not quite right, all Mother had to say was, "Wait until I tell your Daddy about this," and there was instant compliance. I have often wished I could have trained my dog to obey that quickly and well!

Daddy's rules started in the bathroom and, as usual, dealt with the problem of what he perceived as waste. We were allowed to use no more than two sheets of paper for *anything,* so you can bet none was ever wasted. Daddy could be sitting in his rocking chair taking a nap when one of us entered the bathroom and shut the door, which was another rule: when occupied, *close the door.* Don't try to sneak an extra sheet of tissue, because he could hear you and would call out, "Hey, don't use so much paper in there, you're wasting it, *and* you'll stop up the plumbing!" I was never sure which bothered him the most, a possible waste of paper or the possibility something might happen to the plumbing. I decided then that when I was grown up and on my own, I would use as much tissue as I felt necessary.

Now, I absolutely *luxuriate* in being able to use as much or as little as I want. While in my lifetime I may have bought more rolls

Mother and Daddy watching us play, circa 1938.

of toilet paper than Daddy ever did, I have never stopped up the plumbing. From habit, I do still shut the door, and it gives one a wonderful, if fleeting, sense of privacy.

We could turn on no lights other than the room everybody was in, usually the dining-sitting room. Here was Mother's studio couch for resting, and the rocking chair where Daddy read the newspaper or took his naps. Here, too, was the round, golden-oak dining room table made by a Grand Rapids, Michigan, furniture company and styled with Queen Anne legs and matching high-back chairs. A kidney-shaped leather-topped desk stood in front of the twin windows in that room, but no one ever actually sat down there; with no lamp, we couldn't have seen anything anyway. Here, too, was the big floor-model Victrola radio-phonograph where we listened only to selected programs. Electricity was not something to be wasted.

A frosted-glass fixture hung from chains above the table, providing ample light for whatever activity we were engaged in, and during the school year, it was where we all did our homework. When we left that room it was lights-out and bedtime, and those lights were allowed to be on just long enough for undressing and getting into bed. We never had the luxury of reading in bed, something I discovered the joys of many years after I was grown up and away from home. There were no lamps up in our bedrooms, either, just a naked bulb dangling from the ceiling. Reading or studying wouldn't have been at all possible.

Daddy's cardinal rules about food were picked up through osmosis and example. We were never allowed to say, "I don't want any of this" or "I don't like that." It might have been true, but it would have brought Daddy's wrath down on the head of whomever had the temerity to make such a statement. He maintained that whatever was served at the Gordon table was *good* for you, and therefore you must eat it. You could have an additional serving, but you had to take some of everything, not just what you liked.

Daddy served up our plates and seemed to know, down to the last bean, exactly how much each of us normally ate. Didn't finish everything? "You've been eating between meals, haven't you?" he'd ask. That was another no-no, and it usually turned out to be either one of the boys or Leah; I wouldn't have dared to disobey him, except when I'd slipped and bought sliced bologna and bread on the sly. I timed that repast for late afternoon because I knew supper was always a light meal and I could get away with it.

If there was just a teaspoonful of food left over, it had to be saved and refrigerated. The next day Daddy insisted on getting it out and dividing it between *all* of us, himself included. For it not to be eaten would have been wasteful. No one person had to eat the leftovers; it was share-and-share alike, which he said was only fair. Imagine someone dividing five beans or a tablespoon of salad among seven people; then imagine the reality of Daddy actually accomplishing this.

Stanley *hated* spinach, but knew he had to eat it. Daddy would rage at him, "Eat that spinach, boy, *eat* it, it's good for you! Or would a beating help you swallow it?" Poor Stanley, gagging, mouth full, jaws working as he shoveled the spinach into his mouth, tears coursing down his face, would quite woefully shake his head at the beating part, and somehow force himself to clear the last bit from his plate. We had all seen Daddy beat him, yanking him away from the kitchen table and using his belt mercilessly, angry about what he considered Stanley's slowness in downing the spinach. We held our breath whenever it appeared on the table—which, since it was inexpensive, was often—hoping he could make away with his serving. I couldn't bear to hear his cries of pain; it seemed the belt was hitting my own flesh. Yet Mother said not a word, turning a deaf ear and blind eye to the abuse happening right in front of her.

All of us came to hate mealtimes, particularly dinner, for either Stanley or Leah always seemed to be in trouble. For my part, I would eat as quickly as possible, brush any crumbs off my hands, say, "Thank you, Daddy, thank you, Mother," and excuse myself from the table. None of us ever lingered at the table; it was eat and run.

Years later I found out that Daddy didn't really like spinach, either, but ate it because it was supposed to be good for you. He was tickled, positively elated, when he heard about some research reporting that spinach wasn't as good for people as had previously been claimed; it was Daddy's excuse never to eat it again. I always regretted that this research hadn't been reported in time to help poor Stanley. While the rest of us didn't care for spinach either, none of us hated it as much as he did.

It was the rule that Daddy opened the margarine or butter. He very carefully unfolded it so the wrapping didn't tear and, using a knife, scraped the paper clean of any remnants, no matter how minuscule. After all, he had paid for it, and it would be wasteful not to use every single bit of it.

At that time milk was delivered to our home in glass bottles by Eby's Dairy, which was fine in the summer but posed a problem in winter. Since we were all in church, even if we hurried home as soon as services were over, the frozen tops of the milk would be expanded upward and leaning slightly over, like tipsy bowling pins. Daddy, who worked on Saturdays, seemed to take the frozen milk as a personal affront, and would get very angry with Mother about it, insisting one of us should have stayed at home to take in the milk lest the whole bottle be ruined, although he knew full well Mother wouldn't let us stay away from church unless we were sick in bed. This led to many an argument at the dinner table, even though it was the Sabbath—unless of course there were guests, and then Daddy would content himself with glowering at Mother during the entire meal. I was always glad when we had company, for then I didn't have to hear anything.

Daddy did all the grocery shopping, and was so adept at it that he only had to go to market once a week. This also gave him control of the food budget; Mother merely had to cook whatever he purchased. Thursday afternoon was market day, which enabled Mother to cook ahead on Friday for our meals on Saturday, when we could reheat food but do no cooking. Cooking was work, and that was forbidden on the Sabbath; not even the dinner dishes were washed until after sundown and the Sabbath was over. Daddy quite naturally didn't approve of this, but it was one of *Mother's* rules, observed in accordance with her religion.

By this time in our lives we had begun to sense an increasing strain in our parents' relationship over her religion and its observance. Many of their arguments centered on this, and I simply closed my ears to it, for there was nothing I could do or say. Part of Daddy accepted the religion—especially the vegetarianism, the obedience, and the work ethic—but the other part of him warred with it because of his extreme desire for control. Mother was firm in her determination that she would not give in on following what she considered to be God's law. Many times I heard him say, "But the wife is supposed to *obey* her husband!" and Mother would quickly retort, "Only when he isn't contradicting something *God* tells us to do!"

The only physical abuse between them that we ever saw occurred when we were quite small. Mother was, as usual, taking all of us with her to Wednesday night prayer meeting, but for some reason this time Daddy told her she could not go. Mother didn't say anything, just continued putting our snowsuits on us, for it was very cold outside. As we started out the door, Daddy yelled, "Well, if you go, take *all* these little niggers with you and DON'T COME BACK!"

We went anyway and returned home as usual, with Mother putting us all to bed. She knelt beside their big double bed to say her prayers. Daddy, infuriated because she had dared disobey him, reached over, grabbed her arms, and yanked her into the bed, hitting her mouth and cutting her lip in the process. Mother went berserk. With a backhanded grab, she snatched up a solid golden-oak bedside lamp and hit him on the head. Laid it open to the bone. All the fight went right out of him. "Oh, you've *killed* me!" he wailed as he ran to look in the mirror and saw the blood running down his face.

By now we kids, awakened by the ruckus, were standing in the doorway, crying, "Oh, Mother, you've hurt poor Daddy!" Well, *he* was the one with the bloody face, so we thought he was the only victim. Only later did we see blood oozing from the cut on her lip. After a while, Mother got out of bed and took Daddy downstairs to the bathroom, where she reluctantly cleaned and bandaged his wound after shooing us all back to bed. Daddy looked like he had undergone brain surgery.

Of course, the next day at work the ladies at the YWCA teased him unmercifully: "Come on, Bill, tell us what *really* happened. We're willing to bet your wife must have hit you." This was the only time in my life I ever knew Daddy to tell an untruth: "Uh, no, I just got up in the dark to go to the bathroom and walked smack into the bedroom door!" They were only teasing, but they had surely hit the nail on the head.

A few weeks later, when an argument between them began to get rather heated, Daddy hastily said, "Now, now, Camille, we won't have any fighting, let's just sit down and talk calmly about this!" That was the only time he ever laid a hand on Mother for the remaining fifty-eight years of their married life. But he surely could fuss and argue.

3

Daddy Versus Mother Versus Me

MY OWN RELATIONSHIP with my parents was a troubled and ambivalent one, many times crossing back and forth over a very thin line between love and hate. I hated Daddy's treatment of my siblings, yet I could often remain distanced from it while it was happening, almost as though it was occurring in a different time continuum, another place. It might have been selfish of me, but I learned to feel that if it was happening to someone else, that's what was important: try to keep my own nose clean so chastisement didn't come my way.

Had Stanley wet the bed the night before? Many mornings the sounds of a belt hitting bare flesh and his cries of pain awakened us before breakfast. Had he gagged trying to eat spinach at dinner? Instant punishment, right at the table. Often the rest of us children lost our appetites because of the tensions present, but we knew we'd better eat whatever was on our own plates. We began to hate dinnertime for those reasons.

There were many times I also hated Mother because she never spoke up in our defense or remonstrated with him over his unjust treatment. She merely stared blankly at her plate, not even one word issuing from her lips. I failed to understand how she could remain silent under those circumstances, and I often hated her for it.

Our parents were adamant about not living in the "colored" part of town, feeling that living in the "white" part gave them a certain cachet, a status. They cared nothing about the possibility others might think they felt they were better than the average colored person in Elkhart. They did indeed feel superior—in looks, in character, and in actions—all of which in their estimation *did* make them better. They also believed, and frequently expressed at home, their opinion that the colored population was not too clean, either about their persons or in their living conditions: only whites were. These viewpoints were absorbed by the young Gordone, and years later found expression in his drama *No Place to Be Somebody*, when he used the term "clean whites, dirty blacks."

There was also violence that erupted in colored homes and on the streets where they lived; our parents claimed they wished to protect us from that. There is more than one type of violence, however: physical *and* mental. Did they ever consider their actions abuse—physical toward Stanley and Leah, mental and verbal as well—and witnessed by *all* of us in their most extreme manifestations on an almost daily basis? Did that somehow make it a different matter?

I was nearly always around Mother, going everywhere with her, confiding my hopes and aspirations for the future to her. I described my dream wedding to her and my ideal husband. I told her whom I had a crush on and who was interested in me. It didn't take me long to figure out just how to say things to her, for if she didn't like what I was saying or doing, she would tongue-lash me immediately. Often that was as harsh as physical punishment would have been.

When Mother was in the kitchen cooking I was there too, helping her by peeling potatoes, cutting up cabbage, grating carrots for our daily salad, learning how to make flaky pastry dough and biscuits, and in general helping in meal preparation. That's how I learned to cook. During summer vacations from school I prepared dinner every day, and even baked pies from scratch twice a week. I had to make them just like Mother, or Daddy would get upset. (He had a humongous sweet tooth and always expected something delicious for dessert.) Cleaning that seven-room house was also assigned to me, as was doing the ironing for the entire family. Leah was supposed to help, but it was so difficult to obtain her cooperation that it was often quicker and easier to simply do it myself.

Piano practice was Mother's main concern for me; she insisted on an hour in the morning and an hour in the afternoon, with two straight hours on Sunday. Any "spare time" I had was devoted to my beloved books, for I was an avid reader. Most often I would read upstairs and out of sight in my room, for it seemed as though just seeing me sit down with a book in my hands triggered an idea for some different task for me to perform—at once.

All Daddy seemed to require of me was that I be obedient, make good grades in school, do whatever chores around the house Mother assigned, and perform well on the piano. (If I had not done the latter, the money spent on my lessons would have been a waste, and he abhorred waste of *any* kind.) Both of them were never prouder than when I performed perfectly at recital time, with everyone congratulating them on having such an accomplished and talented daughter. How their chests would swell with pride!

Generally, Mother was a different matter altogether. So much more vocal than Daddy, she was never satisfied with my achievements, constantly demanding even greater excellence in everything I did—at home, at school, or at church. I realized at an early age that she was trying to live out her own unfulfilled fantasies of a more accomplished life, expending all her energies in an effort to achieve self-realization vicariously through the achievements of her children. The greatest demands were made on Charles as the eldest son and me as the eldest daughter, upon whom the main thrust of her misguided attempts at self-realization rested. It was demanded that we set a good example for our siblings, and also show the world what *their* children could do.

Charles and I made every effort to live up to Mother's expectations, positive we would be rewarded by her loving us. Collectively and individually, we became utterly confused and devastated when that love was never forthcoming. Instead, we were urged to make even greater strivings toward those pinnacles of perfection that had been drawn up for us. Even our best never seemed quite good enough.

It was Mother's insatiable appetite for greatness and recognition, her demands that we grow up and make her proud of us, that caused us to live in a veritable pressure cooker of effort, conflict, and anguish. I always seemed to be a passenger on an emotional roller coaster.

Daddy seemed more cognizant of my limitations, particularly after my hearing loss, than did Mother. Conversely, the sky was the limit in his expectations for Leah. She had to outdo all of us in school, since she alone was of his blood, which he felt should automatically make her smarter. If she fell short, punishment was immediately forthcoming. Got a B+ in English? Shirley had gotten an A. Got a B- in arithmetic? Shirley or Charles had gotten a B+. The only approval he ever showed Leah was owing to her musical ability, for she performed beautifully on the cello, even playing in the high school orchestra while still in junior high. What enormous pressure this had to have exerted on her young mind! She grew up hating her father, seeing nothing good in him, and eventually extended that hatred to Mother for not protecting her from his cruelty.

The possibility has crossed my mind that perhaps Daddy looked upon me as a near-white child, just as he felt Mother was as near-white as he could possibly hope to marry. His mother died when he was eight, and his father abused him mightily. He ran away from home while quite young and was adopted by a white family in Paris, Tennessee. I'm sure some of his attitudes toward people of different colors and ethnic groups resulted from that family's influence. This might also help explain some of his actions and attitudes toward me, as opposed to his own daughter. But where I was obedient, she was defiant. I was loving; she was indifferent. I tried to obey him; she was rebellious. I wanted to bring him pride and joy; she wanted to do her own thing, and to hell if he liked it or not! She once told me she would do something if she really wanted to, knowing full well she would get a beating for it, for the pleasure would be remembered long after the pain was gone. This I could not understand, for I hated even the threat of physical pain with a passion and would do anything to avoid it.

Summertime was a good and special time for Daddy and me. I was the only child who would wait outside on the back steps to greet him as he rode his bicycle home for lunch. Thursday afternoons, after we had eaten, I went with Daddy to the grocery store to do the week's marketing. He counted on me to remember how much butter we still had, did we have enough carrots, and what about the margarine? I could always answer his questions and loved going to W.W. Wilt's store for our fresh produce and basic supplies like Crisco, sugar, and flour. It was Kroger's for canned goods because they had better prices on those items. Milk was delivered to the house by the local dairy, and he had a standing order for just so many bottles of skim milk, so many of whole milk to use for cooking. He often mixed Pet canned milk with the skim milk in just the right proportions, and he was so expert at it that you couldn't tell the difference from whole-homogenized milk. Hossick's Bakery was on his way home, so he would stop to purchase day-old bread, which he believed better for us than fresh: two loaves of Swedish rye, two of whole wheat, and one loaf of white. Sometimes he would purchase a package of crumb doughnuts because he knew how much I liked them. Special treats were few and far between in the Gordon household!

Every summer I made those trips with him, helping to put the groceries away when we returned home, *after* he checked off the receipts for correctness. In all the years we did this, there was only one time he had been overcharged for an item: thirty-nine cents at Kroger's for a can of peas that should have been twenty-nine cents. Believe me, he immediately went back to collect his dime!

It was during those years that I began to appreciate Daddy's childhood memories. At the dinner table, on his "good" days, he often regaled us with tales of Rin-Tin-Tin, the Wonder Dog of the movies, of Frank "Bring 'Em Back Alive" Buck, big-game hunter who didn't kill animals but brought them back for zoos and circuses. Charles and I listened, mouths agape, to his tales of the exploits of Tom Mix, the cowboy. I think those stories impressed the West on both Charles and me. Every year when the circus came to town, my brothers went to the railroad station early (like 3:00 a.m.!) to help unload animals for later performances, in exchange receiving free entry passes. The rest of us always attended and were amazed at the way the animals were trained to obey. Those were also among the few times we got to eat cotton candy.

Once, when I was about fifteen years old, I had written some poetry and submitted it to a company that advertised in a home magazine, stating they would write music to my "lyrics." The problem was, they wanted thirty-five dollars for my "share of cost," and there was no way that I had that kind of money. None of us kids had ever gotten an allowance, so thirty-five dollars might as well have been $3500. After one of our grocery forays, I told Daddy about the "offer." I almost fell on the floor when he said, "If you want to do it, I'll give you the money."

Daddy the tightwad? Daddy the miser? I couldn't believe it. But I told him I didn't want to take the chance I might not have a "hit" on my hands. All he ever said was, "Well, Shirley, *life* is just a chance!"

And I loved him for his offer. I thought about all the hard work he'd done for the family over the years; fifteen dollars was a week's pay during the Depression and half of the thirty-dollar monthly mortgage on our home. But it proved to me that he, at least, *did* love me, to offer to make that sacrifice.

My major and deepest regret was directed toward both our parents and didn't evolve until my late teens, essentially after Charles had left for the army, which at that time was segregated, and my own college years in Chicago, where the dormitory was also segregated. Segregation was a new situation for both of us. Our parents had been so busy inculcating in us the mores, thoughts, and actions of white people that they neglected to give us an awareness of or sense of pride in our blackness. It took us some time to understand the wonders of Paul Robeson's and Marian Anderson's vocal artistry and not only thrill to it but be proud that I, too, was black like them. Our parents had never commented on or told us about some of the black people right there in Elkhart who had been high achievers in academics, music, and sports, giving us the impression that no black person in Elkhart had ever done anything worthwhile. The only difference, really, had been that we lived in a white neighborhood while most other blacks lived on Elkhart's South Side.

It took some time to overcome those harsh feelings and to process the new knowledge we were gaining. How much of the African American part of our own culture we had missed out on! Mother's recitations of works by Dunbar, Hughes, and so on were only a pale shadow of the riches that were out there, and I had to overcome deep feelings of resentment toward our parents for this deliberate omission and misrepresentation of information about our heritage. It was, in a great sense, the same sins committed by "white" history books toward black people's place in this country's history.

Charles devoted many years of his life to accumulating and studying books about people: French, German, Irish, Hispanic, and

African. Of the more than three hundred volumes in his personal library, more than half dealt with some aspect of African American life. He absorbed a tremendous amount of information, exactly as if he were a human sponge!

Charles ended up spending the rest of his life (after the army) seeking out, understanding, and enjoying the roots of jazz and African American influences and contributions to contemporary performing arts, since he was so actively and vitally involved in the theater. When he was a young man, our Cousin Ora in Chicago used to take him to all of that city's jazz spots and he fell in love with that type of music. The Regal Theatre in Chicago was host to many African American jazz performers, including "Nat" King Cole, "Ivory Joe" Hunter, Ella Fitzgerald, Louis Armstrong, Count Basie, Billy Eckstine, and many others. He never dared tell Mother and Daddy about those excursions, for their religion frowned deeply on any music other than hymns! Well, even that church sang a little gospel or soul music, so the beat went on.

In other vignettes about our parents in this book, you will read in greater detail of other instances where that thin line between love and hate was crossed, back and forth. You, the reader, will be able, I hope, to perceive the different emotions that ebbed and flowed in my mind and heart. Although many things were hurtful and penetrated my very soul, there were also some good things that transpired. For those good things I am grateful and will forever cherish those memories.

4

Our Grandparents

ON DECEMBER 25, 1885, in McKenzie, Tennessee, Nora Gilbert was born, the daughter of a part-colored, part–Native American woman and a Jewish man.

Not far away in Huntingdon, Tennessee, Edward Lee Morgan had been born in the year 1880, also on December 25, the son of a colored woman and a white father. (Grandfather used to say one of his ancestors was Henry Morgan the pirate, but I never knew if he was joking or not.) It was well known in family circles that his ethnic heritage included Irish, Welsh, English, French, and that ultimate drop of blood that in America made him "colored." In South America he would have been considered a white man.

They had met when Grandpa, driving a wagon hitched to a team of mules, drove by Grandma's house on his way to work. Grandma used to run to the front gate and wave to him. One day he simply pulled her onto the wagon seat, took her to a place called Section

House, and married her right then and there. I have the worn and tattered remnants of their marriage certificate, dated October 22, 1899, the writing now faint but still legible. Grandma was almost fourteen and Grandpa was almost nineteen; folks married young in the South. They ended up spending sixty-seven years together, so who's to say teenage marriages don't last?

In 1917 black recruiters were sent to the South to persuade colored people to come north to work on the railroads and in factories, as part of the war effort. Grandma's half-brother, Horace Ingram, came to Elkhart first, then kept urging the Morgans to move there also. He'd gotten a good-paying job with the New York Central Railroad and told Grandpa he could do the same. "Leave the South," he said, "where you'll never be able to make much money or have a chance to do something better for yourself and your family."

Our grandpa had left home when he was only twelve and worked at various odd jobs—including a stint with a railroad, carrying water to the road gangs—so he knew something about "working on the railroad." When Grandpa arrived in Elkhart he, like Uncle Horace, was hired by the railroad to work in the roundhouse, where engines were prepped for the next train out. If any repairs were needed, they were also performed there. It was hard and dirty work that few white men would take on. To be viable, the railroad had to employ whatever labor pool was available.

As soon as he was able, Grandpa sent for Grandma and their four children, since a house had become available at 423 Chapman Avenue. There was no running water or inside toilet facilities, but they hadn't been accustomed to those amenities living in the South, either. As time went on they were able to replace the outhouse with an inside bathroom that had not only hot and cold running water but a commode, a sink, and a bathtub. (I thought this was luxurious:

Grandma and Grandpa Morgan's 1899 marriage certificate *[facing page]*.

WHAT GOD HATH JOINED TOGETHER, LET NOT MAN PUT ASUNDER

THIS CERTIFIES

That Ed Morgan,
of Section house Ky
and [illegible],
of Section house Ky

WERE JOINED TOGETHER BY ME IN THE

BONDS OF HOLY MATRIMONY

At Section house on the 22 — day of
Oct. — in the year of our Lord ~~899~~ 1899

In Presence of

Signed
Rev. W. M. Branham, M. G.

COPYRIGHT, JULY 1st 1886.

our bathroom had only a commode and a tub. Washing up was done using an enameled basin under the faucet of the tub.) Now they could also have running water in the kitchen, and I loved the fact that there was a nice window over the kitchen sink where you could look outside and see other houses, the sky, and trees. It was a real accomplishment when they were able to install a furnace in the basement, for now the entire house could be heated. Since the Morgan family was unaccustomed to the cold of a northern Indiana winter, I'm positive this made a great difference in their ability to enjoy their home.

Grandma was a slim copper-colored woman, about five feet five inches tall, with a beautiful full head of hair that was black like that of her Native American forebears, but softened by a slight wave in it. Her three daughters—Bea, Camille, and Lula—inherited that gorgeous hair, but none of them ever really learned how to wear it except in a bun fastened at the nape of the neck. Grandma had the high cheekbones of her Indian mother, and we all inherited them. Pictures of family members show a strong resemblance around the eyes and those clean features. She was a feisty, free spirit, with a quick tongue and roguish ways.

Grandpa, fair of skin with salt-and-pepper hair and dancing black Irish eyes, had a slow, drawling manner of speaking. They made an arresting couple, although I'm sure Grandma could have stood for a little bit less adoration of Grandpa from the ladies!

From her Indian ancestors Grandma also inherited a love for, and knowledge of, growing things. Her yard on Chapman Avenue became noted for its response to her "green thumb." She had an abundance of roses, and cherry, apple, mulberry, peach, and apricot trees flourished in that rich Indiana soil. In beautifully laid-out flower beds Grandma planted geraniums, cornflowers, bachelor's buttons, carnations, pinks, daisies, cosmos, and moss roses. She seemed to instinctively know the proper place to plant for sun or shade. Grandma loved to share flowers with neighbors and friends, and most Sunday mornings from spring through summer saw her carrying armloads of them up to the St. James African Methodist Episcopal Church, where she was a member, to arrange in vases to decorate the sanctuary. The peony, Indiana's state flower, thrived under her care as in no other yard in Elkhart, with a riot of blooms as large as a person's head, in shades of burgundy, rose, and pale pink.

From her own apple trees she made not only jelly and pies but also sun-dried the sliced fruit in special trays Grandpa made for her. She placed the trays on the flat roof of the back porch and covered them with cheesecloth to keep insects away; then she had Grandpa go up on the roof several times a day to turn the slices so they would dry evenly. When this was accomplished, they were the color of apple butter. Then came a special treat: fried apple pies! She cooked the apple slices into a soft mixture with sugar and a bit of water, then mashed them into a paste and placed several tablespoons apiece onto circles cut from a rich biscuit dough. She folded the circles over into half-moon shapes and then crimped the edges with a fork. After frying them lightly in oil until they were golden-brown on both sides, she placed them on racks to cool. Then Grandma would unfasten the screen door and stand back: she knew we kids could smell them from a mile away and would come bursting into the kitchen to greedily snatch up several at a time. This was one time none of us worried about eating between meals, for we'd already had dinner at noon and since supper was always a light meal, we would make room for that somehow.

No one could make homemade ice cream like Grandma. There were no electric freezers yet, at least not in *her* house, so it was hand-churned from start to finish. After preparing the custard, she poured it into the churn, inserted mixing paddles, and attached the cover, while chipped ice was packed in the space all around. Special "ice cream salt" was sprinkled on the ice (said to make it "colder"), and then the fun started. It was Grandpa's job to turn the crank, and he could tell by the feel of the crank when freezing had been accomplished. The cover was removed, mixing blades taken out, and we could then test the ice cream before everything was repacked with more salt and ice and the whole shebang covered with a small rug kept solely for this purpose.

After setting this aside for a while to "ripen," Grandma would dish up bowls of ice cream for all of us, and what a treat it was! The best-quality milk and finest sugar, with pure vanilla flavors: nothing made today can even begin to compare. This same procedure was followed at our house when Mother made our very own all-natural ice cream; after all, she had learned the method from her own mother.

One summer Grandma was ready to make the first ice cream of the season. Grandpa got the churn down from its storage place in the attic, rinsed it out and dried it, then told Grandma it was ready for her. She followed her regular routine, but this time when the blades were removed and we sampled the ice cream, there was a definitely peculiar flavor, so much so that we couldn't eat it! For some unknown reason, when Grandpa had put the freezer away for the winter he had rinsed the metal-and-wood paddles with kerosene, and the wood had absorbed that flavor. The entire batch had to be thrown out, and we, of course, were devastated. Grandma had to buy another freezer, and she insisted on a White Mountain, the only model she or Mother would use. There was no way to remove the kerosene flavor, but you can believe Grandpa never did that again; he had been just as disappointed as we kids were.

When Grandma went to church she really looked different. She had certain dresses worn only on Sunday, silk stockings (no nylons in those days!), shoes with heels, and a hat. Gloves and a purse completed her attire, for no proper lady went to church or any other social function without these articles of clothing. She would have been thought uncouth or lacking in proper respect for a house of worship. I have a photograph of Grandmother as a young woman, taken with her four children, that commands everyone's admiration because of their sweet facial expressions and the simple beauty of their clothing. The materials and details of their dresses are a totally reflective family portrait and a perfect indication of how one little lady of determination, lacking formal education but highly schooled in common sense and natural refinement, raised a family that so obviously was well cared for. Grandpa was the provider; she was truly his "helpmeet."

Grandma was also famous for her homemade rolls: hot, fragrant, light as a feather, she could never bake enough of them. For holidays and family reunions she baked dozens, but still there were never enough to satisfy everyone. I could have made a meal just from those rolls! While Mother and Aunt Lula could make ice cream like Grandma, they couldn't bake rolls like hers. After years of practice, Aunt Lula came the closest, but she was the first to admit they weren't quite as good as Grandma Morgan's.

Lula moved to California, shortly after which she became the cook and housekeeper for Gene Autry and his wife, Ina. At this time the Autrys lived in the San Fernando Valley at their Melody Ranch location. Both Charles and I visited them when we were in California, for they were very hospitable people. Mr. Autry took us on a tour of the ranch, which was a two-story home with an attached riding ring where he trained his horse to do special tricks for his movies and tours. Stalls were also close by where his horses were kept when not engaged in movie-making or out on tour. Aunt Lula could look from the kitchen windows and watch his maneuvers.

A tanned, trim man, with intensely blue eyes and a warm handclasp, Mr. Autry welcomed us to their home whenever we were in the area. He even showed us the huge room, air-conditioned and with special lighting, where he kept all his Western wear, organized according to shirts, pants, boots, jackets, cowboy hats, and accessories. Charles was particularly interested in seeing all this accumulation of years spent in the saddle. And while Aunt Lula did all the cooking for the Autrys and they were much appreciative of her cooking prowess, she never felt her rolls were as good as Grandma's!

It was customary, back in the 1920s and '30s, to eat chicken every Sunday, and Grandma helped by raising her own. Everything that went with fried chicken was served: creamy mashed potatoes, rich brown gravy, several green vegetables, candied yams, hot biscuits dripping with fresh butter, and homemade pickles and relishes, with several kinds of pie or a fruit cobbler for dessert. Anyone who stopped by the house after church was invited to "set and eat."

The Methodist minister was a Sunday regular. He must have had a built-in alarm clock that signaled him when dinner was being set out on the table. Naturally, when he knocked and was invited in, Grandma would politely ask him to eat with the family. He never refused. Aunt Lula said that on one occasion when she was a young girl, they had eaten down to the last remaining piece of chicken on the platter, which the minister reached for at the same time as she did. Huffily, she told him, "Go right ahead and take the last piece for your own greedy self!"

Although he gave an embarrassed laugh, he *did* take it, and Aunt Lula got a reprimand for being rude to company. "Company, Mama?" she sassily queried. "That man ain't company, he eats 'most as many meals at this table as *we* do!"

The minister didn't have to be divinely advised to know which of his parishioners were the best cooks and set the most sumptuous tables. We speculated that he made "rounds" to other homes during the week, saving Grandma's house for Sunday.

I remember one time, when asking the blessing as usual, after a lengthy oration the minister said, "And bless the hands that prepared this food. Now pass me down that chicken, please!"

Grandma always had on a freshly ironed cotton housedress with a crisply starched apron over it. We never saw her in a robe in the kitchen; she was always fully dressed with her hair brushed and combed when she came downstairs to put on the coffee pot and prepare breakfast. I've noticed this same habit among women who have worked as domestics: early risers, early dressers, and early to bed.

Morgan children: Lula (*front center*), Camille, Algie (*second row, left to right*), Bea (*back row*), 1914.

We were not allowed to spend the night any place except at our grandparents' house. It was Daddy's rule: you sleep in your own bed, at home, at night. Of course, we weren't invited to the white kids' slumber parties, but we preferred our grandparents' home anyway. The Saturday nights we spent there became a family "fun" tradition we never forgot, and certainly never got enough of. For a long time it was all five of us over there; then, with the passing years, the boys outgrew the bed we had all slept in, so the three of them would spend the night on occasion, while Leah and I, the two girls, would stay there together. In those days before mixes, packaged goods, and microwaves, who else but a grandmother would fix as many freshly made pancakes or waffles as five hungry and greedy kids could eat? With homemade maple syrup, yet?

Grandpa always called Grandma "the workin'est woman I ever saw in my life." She scrubbed the kitchen floor on her hands and knees daily; it was so clean you could almost eat off it. Windows were washed frequently, and carpets were hung outdoors on the clothesline at least twice a year and beaten to within an inch of their life with a paddle-shaped wire contraption called, appropriately, a "rug beater." Silver was kept shining and polished all the time. Her "good" china was perpetually washed, dried, and put back into the "Chin'ey" cabinet immediately; no dust would have had either the chance or the effrontery to land on it. And Grandpa spent a lot of time away from home during those two periods of cleaning frenzy, fall cleaning and spring cleaning. That was a time of madness all its own.

Most of Grandma's early cleaning supplies were of her own concoction: vinegar and newspapers for cleaning windows and glass; brown bar soap for laundry *and* bath, made in a black kettle set on bricks in the backyard and "cooked" over a wood fire. That stuff would almost remove paint, not to mention what it did to one's skin! Even in later years Grandma never had much faith in store-bought cleaners and such. Add ammonia and baking soda to the above list, and you could clean anything.

Every scrap of material eventually found its way into one of two bags—one to be used for quilting pieces, the other for use as cleaning rags. All buttons were removed from worn-out or outgrown clothing, from Grandpa's drop-seat long johns to each blouse, skirt, shirt, or dress that could no longer be worn. The buttons were stored in quart jars to be used in her sewing or whenever a button needed

Camille, Grandma, Bea (*front row, left to right*),
Lula, and Algie (*back row, left to right*), 1918 [*facing page*].

replacement. I learned how to darn socks sitting at Grandmother's knee; no sock would ever be discarded because of such a minor thing as a hole.

Grandpa swore up and down that the lace window curtains wore out just from being washed so often. She had a movable wooden frame set up by Grandpa to lean against the house, with adjustable bolts and little nails all around the edges of it, to which she pinned the edges of the curtains, leaving them to dry in the sun. Set up this way, they didn't need ironing, just careful handling to avoid creases before they were rehung at the windows. It was necessary to do this early in the morning to avoid the soot belching from the roundhouse a couple of blocks away. Grandpa would groan when she'd tell him she needed him to put this apparatus up: "Oh, not agin, Nora, you jes' did this t'other day!" He did it anyway, for he knew grumbling would get him nowhere.

Even the ceilings, walls, and floors did not escape her sharp eyes. With a scarf wrapped around her head and a piece of dampened cloth fastened around the end of her broom, Grandma attacked dust and dirt with equal impunity. No spiderwebs or dust balls, ever, not in *her* house—not in any nook or cranny, or under any bed or piece of furniture.

She often proclaimed, "Soap and water is two of the cheapest things they is, and you kin be poor, and you kin be raggedy, but you *and* the rags kin be *clean!*" Her personal covenant with God was simply expressed: "Lawd, I won't tell You what to do, jes' bless me n' mine, and I'll set 'em up afore You as clean as I can get 'em, inside and out." It worked for her.

Grandma had her white ladies for whom she cleaned during the day, then brought their laundry home to do. In inclement weather, she boiled the linens in a big copper wash boiler on the wood-burning stove on the enclosed back porch; when the weather was clear, she used a huge, black, cast-iron three-legged kettle set up on bricks outside. (Washing machines were still uncommon, even among the wealthy.) After being laundered and then dried on the clothesline, dozens of white linen tablecloths with matching napkins, and acres of sheets and pillowcases with fancy borders, had to be ironed, which was yet another major undertaking. Everything had to be sprinkled down with water, rolled up so the moisture would dissipate evenly, then carefully guided over the board with her iron swiftly flashing and folded precisely so they went into a special basket and never touched the floor.

I smile today when I hear women complain about the work involved in having to "do the laundry"; with automatic washers, dryers, and permanent press fabrics, very little if any ironing is required. They don't know what it means to actually *work* at doing the laundry. The hardest part nowadays is in sorting the clothes, then deciding which button to push!

I think it was working in these wealthy white folks' homes that further developed Grandma's innate sense of quality home furnishings and love of "good" things. How she enjoyed fine linens, porcelain and china, and well-designed furniture. The things she bought back then would be collector's items and antique dealers' dreams in today's market: Aubusson and Oriental carpets, Tiffany lamps, an upright Steinway piano, sterling silver tea service sets, Lennox china, Fostoria and Waterford crystal. During her lifetime, she hand-stitched a staggering number of quilts. A Strauss Austrian crystal chandelier hung from the ceiling over the dining room table, sparkling like diamonds; it was taken down regularly, carefully dismantled piece by piece, washed in ammonia and water, then just as carefully hand-dried, reassembled, and hung back up in place. She began collecting Depression glass before most people realized what it was or how desirable it would be. All this from a woman who'd had no formal education, was scarcely able to write her name, and who never made more than two dollars a day working.

We used to tease her, saying she'd inherited her natural thriftiness not only from the Indians, but also from her Jewish father.

Grandma used to tell us of her childhood days in the South, where she grew up doing whatever work she could put her young hands to. While the slaves had been freed a quarter-century before she was born, many of them had no place to go and no work they were trained for, so they and their children continued to work in the cotton fields for "shares," a roof over their heads, and whatever cash money the whites would condescend to pay them. Grandma was reputed to be just about the fastest cotton picker for miles around, even though she was so very young.

Her stepfather, Grandpaw Ingram, *had* been a slave, but after freedom came and his son Horace had moved to Elkhart, it wasn't long before he too moved north. He lived right across the street from the roundhouse, in a tiny house on Wagner Avenue surrounded by a huge lot that he'd planted with a garden. He was a small, wizened man; we kids never understood how he could ever have been a slave, for he just didn't seem big or strong enough. He often spoke of working in the cotton fields, so perhaps his short stature was an asset: the closer you were to the ground, the better reach you had! He lived to be 107, so evidently hard work hadn't hurt him.

Grandma was also noted for her ability, as a youngster, to ride and handle horses and mule teams; this must have been inherited from her Indian ancestors and genetically passed down to her grandson Charles, for in later years he was a great horse lover and could ride like the wind. In truth, Charles and I both inherited a love for open spaces, animals, and nature, which we felt was part of our Native American heritage. Years later, we were in complete agreement that nothing could compare with a gallop in the early morning, when dawn is just breaking and all you can see for miles are trees, wildflowers, and blue mountains on the far horizon, and the only sound is your horse's hooves beating upon the ground. No need for words: our expressions said it all!

Now, Grandpa was a huntin' man. (Show me a man from Tennessee or Kentucky who *can't* shoot a rifle, and I'll seriously doubt his antecedents!) Squirrels and rabbits seemed to wait just to jump in front of his gun or surrender to his hunting dogs. He always had between eight to twelve dogs in a run at the far end of the yard: bluetick hounds, coonhounds, redbone hounds. On nights when the moon was full you could hear them baying from blocks away. Grandpa would get out of bed and go talk to them, and they settled right down. Naturally Grandma could and did cook up the tastiest fried squirrel with gravy or rich rabbit stew that you'd ever want to sop a biscuit into, and Grandpa made sure she had plenty to work with. Hunting was a steady source of meat for the Morgan family table and a source of pride for Grandpa: his nickname among fellow hunters was "Ol' Eagle-Eye Ed." We Gordon kids were glad we were vegetarians and never had to face rabbits, deer, and squirrels on our plate; we couldn't even stomach the thought!

Sometimes we'd find Grandpa sitting out by the dog runs talking to them—not much, just enough so his dogs knew the sound of his voice and the meaning of various whistles and signals he gave. "You don't want to cozen a huntin' dog much, or you'll spile 'em for huntin," he'd drawl. "They won't know if you want 'em to play or work, so best be firm in your dealin's with 'em." (I think this was also his philosophy in raising his children.)

Only a few dogs went out hunting at a time, at the most two or three, but we knew his favorite was a small black-and-tan beagle, Lady. He preferred her because, he swore, "She *thinks* like a dadgummed rabbit or squirrel, and knows which way they'll be runnin' afore they know it theyselves!" This was high praise indeed from a huntin' man.

In their later years our grandparents took turns visiting their three children in California, spending a month or two at a time. (The West had a strong pull on the whole Morgan family; their son, Al, and two daughters, Bea and Lula, moved there. All of the Gordon kids except Cecil eventually lived in California.) As a retired railroad man, Grandpa could always get a pass for either of them.

One particular year, it was Grandma's turn to make the trip. While she was gone, Grandpa cut down the three catalpa trees that had stood and bloomed for years on their corner of Chapman and Delaware. Charles used to pull the seed pods from those trees to make pretend sabers for mock fights with his brothers. Every year I looked for their mass of blooms, which looked like God had stuck a gigantic bouquet into the ground. Without them, that corner looked positively naked.

Of us all, only Charles had the temerity to ask Grandpa why he had done this. "Them trees is too messy!" he curtly replied, the tone of his voice and the tautness of his facial muscles letting Charles know the conversation was over and he didn't want to hear anything further about it. But we knew there would be more to hear when Grandma returned.

Sure enough, she cried, she wailed, she even said a whole string of swear words, until she realized nothing she could say or do would bring those trees back. In her Native American book, you *never* destroyed nature, you nurtured it. After a time, Grandma seemed to become her usual animated self, although we often noticed her glances drifting through the kitchen window as she washed the dishes, coming to rest on the spaces previously occupied by those trees. She seemed actually to mourn their loss.

The following year it was Grandpa's turn to go to California, and we all saw him off at the train depot. I guess we weren't really surprised when, one day shortly thereafter, Charles came running to tell us: "Grandma has gotten rid of *all* of Grandpa's hunting dogs!" We rushed over to their house and sure enough, the runs were not only empty, but even the dog houses and feeding bowls were gone. She'd had no trouble getting rid of them, for they all were well trained, and if someone really wanted a dog but had no money to pay for one, why, she simply *gave* them a dog, cautioning them never to tell anyone.

The only dog that remained was a household pet, a black cocker spaniel named Judy Ann. We knew a payday would be coming when Grandpa got back home, and while we were anxious and glad to see him, we knew he would be heartsick at the loss of his beloved dogs. We couldn't even speculate what form his anguish would take.

"You're too old to go out huntin' anymore," was the reason she gave Grandpa when he confronted her upon his return, trembling with rage. As they say, "Oh my, the fur did fly!" He didn't hit her, but we could see he surely *wanted* to. There was quite a noticeable rift between them for a long, long time, but eventually they did make their peace. From that time on, their California trips were always made *together.*

One summer, their eldest daughter Bea had come from California on vacation. Mother, Grandma, and Bea were sitting in the swing on the front porch, and Grandpa was in his favorite rocking chair, in easy spitting distance for his chewing tobacco. Aunt Bea had just been berating Grandpa for coming home "under the influence" the night before. Grandpa angrily jumped up from his rocker, ran out to his old Ford, put it in gear, and promptly reversed himself into a tree. He didn't even wait to assess any damage—just shifted gears, jammed on the accelerator, and took off down the street, tires spinning up a cloud of dust. The adults on the porch were laughing so hard they couldn't run to the street fast enough to stop him. But now that I think of it, that was the last time I ever saw Grandpa drive.

The neighborhood kids loved to hang around Grandpa. He had plenty of time since he was retired, as well as lots of patience with their questions and many stories of his boyhood with which to regale them. Their eyes opened wide when he told them how he'd run away from home when he was twelve to go to work on the railroad, taking water to the roadbed gangs, and how after moving to Elkhart, he'd gotten a job working in the cinder pit at the roundhouse. He explained how, when the engines came in, it was his job to empty out the clinkers, stoke up the boiler, and ready the engine for the next train. "Gee, you must have been a pretty important fella, Mr. Morgan," they exclaimed, which tickled him immensely. I don't think anyone had ever told him that before.

One night at work in the mid-1930s, Grandpa climbed into the firebox of an engine, all set to remove the clinkers. They were supposed to be "dead," but weren't, and he suffered massive burns, which in turn became infected and prevented him from returning to work again. So the railroad retired him on disability pay, giving him a pension and a gold watch. How he treasured that watch! He would pull it from his vest pocket, for he wore it constantly, and show it to the children, pointing out the train engraved on the back of its case. He told them stories of the crack speed of the famous old Engine 999, of the super-luxury of the Twentieth-Century Limited, which had only three stops between Chicago and New York, with Elkhart being the first one. He spoke of how all the movie stars and famous personages rode the Limited, which back then was the fastest and most luxurious way to get to New York City. They listened with ears and eyes wide open at his stories of other engines he'd worked on, back in the days of coal-fired trains that could reach great speeds. When the 3:00 p.m. quitting whistle blew at the roundhouse, he'd check the watch for accuracy, and it was always right. They surely made good watches back then, for his Elgin kept perfect time up until he died in 1966 at the age of 86.

Grandma loved music; often, while working in the kitchen, she would hum some long-ago-and-far-away tune that sounded more like an Indian chant than it did either old-time slavery songs or church hymns. Charles learned to sing many of them simply by listening to her. She was especially proud of her grandchildren's musical accomplishments: Charles's beautiful tenor voice; Stanley's "fiddlin'," as she called it; my piano playing; and Leah's cello-playing ability. She had never seemed to recognize that her own daughter, Camille, had a lovely soprano voice; *we* were her grandchildren and as such deserved special recognition on her part.

Grandma and Grandpa Morgan's sixtieth wedding anniversary, 1959.

Grandma accompanied my parents to every program, every recital, and every performance she could. She would proclaim to everyone within earshot, a proud smile on her face, "You know, that's my gran' chile," or if, as often happened, more than one of us appeared on the same program, "Yessir, them's *my* gran' chillen!" Mother always maintained that neither she nor her siblings had gotten that much attention or approval when *they* were growing up. I've often thought this might have been because Grandma was so young when she married and started her family; she was preoccupied and busy growing up at the same time as her children. Leah and I often said we too were going to get married when we were thirteen, just like Grandma, but thank God we didn't. We were not that mature at that age, and couldn't have handled either a husband or children at such a tender age!

Grandma was a strict disciplinarian, a firm believer that if you spared the rod (first choice: peach-tree switches), you would spoil the child. Backed up always by Grandpa, she had ruled her own progeny with an iron hand, and they had a very narrow path to tread, for her primary maxim was "Chillen is to be seen, not heard." Yet she never had to spank any of her grandchildren, either Mother's five or Aunt Lula's two, and always seemed bewildered when she heard about a spanking or beating one of us had gotten. I can see her now, a frown creasing her brow and lips drawn taut, muttering, "Twarn't necessary, I know twarn't necessary."

We felt so secure in the love of both grandparents—an unconditional love—that for us 423 Chapman Avenue was a haven of love, peace, and refuge. It seemed that grandchildren were just what God had ordered for Grandma. A small embroidered pillow I saw the other day made me smile, for it really summed things up nicely: "If I'd known grandchildren were so much fun, I'd have had them first!" The love emanating from both of them was undoubtedly what drew us to flee to them when things became unbearable at home.

I remember Grandma on all the festive occasions of our lives, separate and apart from our musical performances. Besides the Thanksgiving and Christmas holidays, there were summertime picnics and trips to the beach at Lake Michigan, to the zoo and the amusement park, to the World's Fair in Chicago, even to various local parks to enjoy the greenery, the flowers, and the river. We went to band concerts in the park in the summer, and Grandma always brought a blanket to spread on the grass under a tree, where all of us sprawled while enjoying the sound of the river's rippling currents as well as the rousing band music.

It was Grandma who always took the time to explain certain facts of life to us: why we shouldn't go into the field on Uncle's farm where a large bull was in residence; why we should be very careful when climbing out the bedroom window on the second floor to clandestinely (we thought) pick cherries off the tree; how to go down a country road and locate sassafras bushes and dig their roots to make a "spring tonic"; why we shouldn't go out into the far section of her yard in our white dress shoes when the mulberries were ripe (she was right; those stains couldn't be polished out!); why we should always close (not slam) the screen door behind us in the summertime: besides the obvious loud noise that was jarring to the ear, it was so her "pet" flies couldn't get out, naturally. Everything had its reason and its season, and she was a veritable fount of information on the whys and wherefores of so many things.

One of the first examples of her unconditional and forgiving love for her grandchildren occurred during a visit to Potawatomi Park, located between Osceola and Mishawaka, as I recall. Our parents, Grandmother, and Cousin Ora had taken us to see an exhibit of buffalo. The boys were about two, three, and four; I was only one, so Mother carried me. Charles, standing next to Grandma, was awed by the tremendous bulk and size of these beasts, one of whom was munching on some hay right next to the fence. Suddenly, the bull stamped his hoof and snorted, and the startled Charles jumped about a foot in the air, unfortunately landing right on Grandma's sore corn. She yelled out in pain. That bull took off running to the back of the park and wouldn't come out the rest of the time we were there.

I call this "unconditional and forgiving love" on Grandma's part, for as soon as the pain subsided she swept Charles up in an embrace and murmured, "There, now, honey, I *knows* you didn't go and do that on purpose!" Telling us this story at a later time, Cousin Ora seemed able to make her face a perfect reflection of Charles's surprise and Grandma's pain. Even though Grandma swore, "Twarn't funny!" she too had to join in the laughter.

I particularly loved the quiet orderliness of Grandma's home. Everything was in its place, clean and shining. Yet, as busy as she was, she had time to relax on the porch swing in summer, indoors in her rocking chair in winter. Most important, she always had time for us.

It seems quite incredible that two people almost totally lacking in formal education could figure out what their grandchildren needed to gain emotional and mental maturity. They accomplished this through their tremendous love for us, not expressed so much in words as through actions, and it enshrined them forever in our hearts.

5

Hudson Street

WHEN MOTHER MARried William Gordon she already had four children close in age to each other, for we had all been born within a five-year period.

The first thing Daddy did was move his new family away from the South Side, where we had all lived with our grandparents, and well away from those demarcation lines of the railroad tracks, into a completely white neighborhood on Elkhart's northwest side. Daddy refused to live around other colored people, and this move from the South Side was his personal statement that he considered living among them unacceptable. To us kids, at that age, it was simply where we lived, and therefore we had no knowledge of his motivations for the move.

This is the very first place in which I remember living. A two-story white clapboard house, it had an open sun porch on the upper floor with a balustrade around it and French doors that opened from our parents' bedroom, which became a place we could sit in the hot summer evenings and try to catch a cool breath of air. Unfortunately, like most of the Midwest, during the heat of summer it could be as hot at midnight as it was at noon, the only difference being that the sun had set.

An oval glass pane was set in the front door, its beveled edges reflecting a rainbow of colors in the light. I promptly walked right through this glass, which reached almost from the top to the bottom of the door, breaking it into a hundred pieces. I didn't even get a scratch.

A wide staircase rose from the foyer to the second floor and led to a small hallway, the master bedroom, and the bath. Charles, Stanley, and I shared the only other bedroom, while Cecil continued to live with our grandparents on Chapman Avenue: space was definitely at a premium. Besides, Grandma said her house felt empty and lonely with her own children long since grown and gone, so she welcomed having a grandchild to look after.

There was a tiny yard enclosed by a small white picket fence, and wonder of wonders, there was green grass growing all around. It amused Daddy that, even in the midst of this white neighborhood, ours was one of the few yards with grass.

There was just about enough space for us to play outside, but to us as small children it seemed quite spacious. In winter, when snow piled up into immense drifts and Mother had warmly wrapped us up against the cold, we loved making snow forts, snowballs, and snow angels. Charles was always the ringleader in those games, for he could hit any of us with an unerring eye for accuracy.

The Hudson Street house seemed to be a place of accidents for me, for in addition to breaking that glass on the front door, I stood up in—and fell out of—my high chair onto the kitchen stove, which fortunately wasn't hot at the time. On yet another occasion I tumbled down the basement steps, landing on my head. Mother said it sounded just like a ripe watermelon because I still had no hair; it didn't start growing until I was about three years old. (The expression Charles used to describe me was "bald as a goose's egg.")

During one subzero cold spell, Mother gathered all of us kids downstairs around the floor register of the furnace to put our clothes on. It was too cold to even *think* about doing this upstairs, so I brought my little potty downstairs rather than risk freezing my backside off. Charles, ever the tease, thought it funny to grab hold of the potty so I couldn't sit on it. With my drop-seat pajamas flapping, I yanked it back. All of a sudden he let go; I lost my balance and landed on my bare backside on the *very* hot floor register. The pattern it embossed was visible for some time, while Charles in turn got a spanking that not only warmed *his* seat but, I'm sure, made quite an impression on him!

One day a neighbor, screaming and wringing her hands, rushed to the basement where Mother was doing laundry. "Oh, Mrs. Gordon, come quick! Charles is walking around on the upstairs railing, and I'm so afraid he's going to lose his balance and fall and break his neck!"

Mother dropped everything, taking the basement stairs two at a time and drying her hands on her apron as she ran, followed closely by the neighbor. Both were frightened half to death at what they might find. She later said she didn't want to startle Charles by making any sudden noises or yelling at him, so as she neared the French doors that were opened wide to the outdoors, she began humming a tune. Stepping outside, she could scarcely believe her eyes: her five-year-old son was indeed doing a skillful balancing act as he traversed the railing, arms fluttering in midair like bird's wings as he placed one foot in front of the other.

When Mother got close enough to grasp Charles firmly she did so, hanging on to him for dear life, and they both sank to the floor for a moment as she waited for her heartbeat to return to some semblance of normal. Charles was bewildered by the abrupt end to his acrobatics, for Mother's arms were clasped around him as tightly as a vise. "I can do that!" he insisted, struggling unsuccessfully to free himself. "Besides, I've done it before!" The neighbor lady could only shake her head, but she did witness the seat-warming Mother gave him after making him solemnly promise never to do such a thing again.

The neighbor who reported Charles's act of derring-do, Mrs. Ruby Kendall, was white, a very kind and friendly woman with five children of her own who seemingly harbored no prejudices about having colored neighbors and treated us all with lovingkindness. I'm sure her own family kept her busy, but the milk of human kindness flowed strongly in her veins. She could have let that colored family watch out for their own kids, but she was too much of a humanitarian to see someone in danger and not come to their aid.

Her children also did her proud; one son, Roger, became one of Elkhart's most beloved police officers. Two daughters, Lauraine Holycross and Charlene Potterbaum, became a nurse and published author, respectively. Even after we all moved to different homes and locations, the girls and their mother frequently invited me to come over and play the piano for them. This was one family whose sincere regard for all of us we never once doubted.

I was three when our baby sister, Leah Geraldine, was born at Elkhart General Hospital. A lady whom we called "Aunt Jo" came over while Mother was gone, to fix our meals, dress us, and supervise our playtime, since it was February and there was a lot of snow outside. I've always remembered Aunt Jo as the one responsible for making me hate macaroni and cheese for a mighty long time. I don't know what she did, but it tasted absolutely awful. We had no choice, either, for Daddy was firm in making us eat whatever was set in front of us. We learned quite early that protesting we "didn't like" something was of no use whatsoever; we ate it anyway.

Aunt Jo died when I was about seven, my first experience with death, and I remember attending her funeral up at Canaan Baptist Church. I looked at her, gowned in a pretty peach-colored lace dress, crystal beads around her neck, holding a matching spray of gladiolus in her hands—and all I could think of was, "Well, God sure won't be asking *you* to make macaroni and cheese up in heaven!"

But when I had first met Aunt Jo, it was an exciting time because of Leah's arrival—a new baby and a girl at that—even though no one told me about it beforehand. Mother had related to me the story of how, when I was born, she had been disappointed because I was a girl. Since she already had three boys, she wanted me to be a boy too. When Grandma told her she'd just had a girl, Mother cried, "Oh no, I don't want a girl, I want a boy!" and Grandma asked, "Must I throw her out the window, then?" (She could ask that, since I had come into the world just like my brothers Stanley and Cecil, delivered in her upstairs front bedroom.) But Mother's younger sister, Lula, stepped forward and begged, "Oh, Camille, she's the cutest little thing—if you don't want her, give her to me!"

Years later Mother qualified her remark upon that occasion by explaining, "No, if I was dirty enough to get you, I'm dirty enough to keep you." Older, I took it to indicate she'd been brought up with the belief that sex was dirty, a lesson commonly taught to young girls in those days by their very own mothers, with unmarried pregnancy at the very top of their no-no list. Regardless of her reasons, I was very happy she had decided to keep me. Mother seemed quite content that Leah was a little girl, explaining, "Now you won't be the only girl in the family."

Comfortably ensconced in the big double bed upstairs, Mother and Leah were taking life easy. I wanted to see my baby sister, but most of all I wanted to be assured Mother was really and truly back home, for she had never left us before. Aunt Jo forcibly kept me downstairs. Every time I tried to climb the stairs, she would come after me. In desperation, I tried to quietly sneak up there, but I was still so small I had to climb up step by step on my hands and knees. When I was almost at the top, I felt myself lifted from behind and carted back downstairs. Frustrated, I started crying.

"What's the matter, Jo Ella?" Mother called out.

"Oh, she keeps trying to come upstairs and I don't want her bothering you and the baby, you need to rest," Aunt Jo replied.

"Well, it's all right, let her come on in," Mother said, and I shot like a rocket into that front bedroom and clambered up onto the bed where Mother was holding and nursing Leah. How tiny the baby seemed! Mother put one free arm around me, and I cuddled up, content at last, for I could see and touch her. The three of us had a quiet visit until, worn out with my attempts to scale those stairs, I fell sound asleep, along with Leah and Mother.

I could tell Aunt Jo didn't like having been overruled. I later found out that she wasn't really any blood relation to us, not an aunt after all. I therefore felt quite justified in not being too fond of her, especially since she made such bad-tasting macaroni and cheese. I remember quite clearly that once Mother was up and about, she prepared the same dish and we all loved it. I now think it must have been Aunt Jo's cheese choice . . . it definitely wasn't the same brand Mother used, which made all the difference in a child's world.

6

Pearl Street

WE LEFT HUDSON Street shortly after Leah was born. Our new home was on Pearl Street, between Tenth and Eleventh streets, almost in the center of the Italian part of town. Oh, it was a wee house! There were only two bedrooms: one for our parents, with Leah tucked into her crib in one corner, while Charles, Stanley, and I slept in the other in a huge cast-iron bed that had been painted a shocking pink, although some of the paint had been chipped off. It took up almost the entire room. The dining room was small, with a coal-burning Franklin stove at one end. I remember Mother using stove blacking on the pipe and putting up a decorative tin plate where it entered the wall. With no furnace, the whole house had only this stove to heat it. I loved watching the flames dance in that old stove through its isinglass windows.

All the kids were interested in the novelty of watching Mother feed the baby, especially at breakfast, which was usually oatmeal followed by orange juice containing a jolt of cod-liver oil. I wondered why my brothers always seemed to disappear after Leah had her oatmeal, until I found that just by being in Mother's sight, I could count on a glass of orange juice for myself—and I loved that—but at the bottom of the glass would be that nasty cod-liver oil. Heavier than the juice, it always sank to the bottom, and it was always the last swallow. *Ugh!* For years afterward I was unable to drink orange juice without expecting to taste that stuff. Quite soon I learned to conveniently join my brothers in another room, or even outdoors, when it was juice time. So much for togetherness.

It was on Pearl Street I had my tonsils removed, and Pearl Street where we all came down with the usual childhood diseases. Charles, being the oldest and already attending school, would invariably be the one who first brought home the germs of chicken pox, measles, and whooping cough, and so generously shared them with the rest of us. Even Cecil wasn't immune: he was exposed to it all on his regular visits when he came to play, and then had to stay put and suffer. How on earth did Mother survive with five of us simultaneously itching, scratching, or coughing all at the same time or within a few days of one another? It seemed when one child was recovering, another would start.

We were quite fascinated to discover that most of our Italian neighbors not only had fantastic vegetable gardens but also kept a goat or two. Sometimes they would let us get up close and watch them milk. We clustered around Nanny and examined her from quite a few different angles as we tried to figure out why her "faucet" didn't have a handle on it. While we didn't care for the taste of goat's milk, the mechanics of obtaining it completely absorbed us. Finally, Charles *had* to try his hand at it, but those young fingers couldn't quite work their magic on Nanny, and after old "Billy" butted in a few times Charles gave it up as a bad job. That's one of the few times I remember him not being successful at something he tried so hard to do.

"Nigger"

Most of the Italian parents in our neighborhood had come over from the "old country," and they spoke only broken English. But they and their children did know the word *nigger.* For a time Mother made excuses for them: "Perhaps they simply don't know very many English words." Daddy looked at her and snorted, "Well, maybe not, but they already speak enough English to get by in *this* country!"

The D'Angelo family lived right next door to us, and Mother thought it would be nice if I could play with their daughter Anna Maria, even though she was closer to Charles's age. In those days, girls played separately from boys. I was out on the front porch one day shortly after we moved into the neighborhood. Anna was also on her porch, so I called over to her, "Hi!" She stared at me and hollered back, "Nigger!"

Puzzled, I went inside to ask Mother what *nigger* meant, for never before had I heard that word. Her exact words were: "You go back out there and tell her *she's* a *wop!*" Oops! I could tell then that *nigger* and *wop* mustn't be very nice words, but obediently I went back outside and called out, "You know what you are?"

She started screaming "No! No! No!" and holding her hands over her ears. Emboldened by Mother's instruction, I yelled, "You're nothing but a bowlegged, bow-diddly *wop!*" before wheeling around and going back inside, extremely proud of my ability to do what Mother had told me to, even slamming the screen door behind me for emphasis.

Quiet reigned for about twenty minutes, then Mother and I heard calls of "Nigger, nigger, nigger!" Mother glanced out of the kitchen window, but seeing nothing she continued washing dishes at the sink. Again we heard, "Nigger, nigger, nigger, come here, nigger!" Mother's face turned beet-red, and every freckle on her face stood out as though carved in bas-relief. She stormed out of the kitchen, through the dining room, and across the porch before coming to a militant standstill at the D'Angelos' front door and *knocking.* I thought it prudent to stay on our front porch—making sure, however, I could hear everything that was said.

Mrs. D'Angelo came to her front door. "Who are you calling *nigger?*" Mother demanded, fire in her eyes and fight written all over her body. "Oh, dog's name, dog's name!" Mrs. D'Angelo exclaimed, pointing to a little black dog who had followed her to the door and was standing there wagging his tail.

Mother looked down skeptically at the animal. "Oh, you don't say?" she queried. "Well, I've never seen that dog before, and I really think you should change its name or get rid of it. NOW. Cause if you don't, *I'll* have to do it *for* you!" Not waiting for a reply, Mother turned on her heel and marched back into the house. As I stood there, mouth agape, she tossed her head defiantly and said, "Hmph, I'll bet that's *one* English lesson she understood and won't forget in a hurry!"

We never again heard any further calls for "Nigger," nor did we ever see the little dog again. This was my first experience in seeing Mother's wrath, and I was quite vividly impressed. If she was going to be angry with someone, I surely hoped it would not be me!

Not long afterward Mother and Mrs. D'Angelo actually became friends, at least to the extent that they talked over the back fence while hanging out the laundry. Mrs. D'Angelo even invited us over to sample some freshly baked Italian bread, still warm and crusty from the oven. I could have eaten the whole loaf. One day she offered us a taste of some steamed snails she was preparing for lunch, but Mother and I politely turned down what was obviously a delectable treat—for them.

Years later I discovered Anna became a nun, and I've often wondered if she ever remembered the little colored girl or the black puppy once called "Nigger."

Little Italy stretched from our street up to, over, and around Harrison Street. There were a few neighborhood stores specializing in Italian foodstuffs that emitted tantalizing aromas of cheeses, meats, sauces, and sausages as you walked by. A couple of restaurants, small but neighborhood-friendly, were scattered throughout the area, their checkered red-and-white tablecloths topped with raffia-wrapped wine bottles holding glowing candles that fairly called out, "Come in!" Money was scarce for nearly everyone, and dining out wasn't on the Gordons' menu.

I've since wondered if they would have served us if we had been bold enough to go in. They might have, for they did accept us relatively easily into the neighborhood with only a few isolated incidents. Those were mostly times when Charles had to prove to the Italian boys that he could and would fight any of them, even if they were bigger than he was. This was usually provoked by Cecil, on one of his frequent visits, proclaiming loudly to one and all that *his* big brother could lick any of *their* big brothers. After Charles proved he wasn't afraid of a fight—not looking for one, yet never backing down from a direct confrontation and even winning several—he was let alone and accepted as just another good kid in the neighborhood.

The Clubhouse

A ramshackle weather-beaten shed with warped grey boards, no paint, and a dirt floor stood in our backyard on Pearl Street. It didn't take Charles long to organize the boys in the neighborhood to form a club, complete with warning signs posted on the rickety door: "BOYS ONLY!" "NO GIRLS ALLOWED!" "KEEP OUT! THIS MEANS ALL GIRLS!" Quite naturally all the girls wanted to go in, but lacked the nerve. One of my playmates, a girl named Violet who lived across the alley, and I were simply dying to enter.

Charles adamantly refused to allow this, posting one of the boys at the door whenever they were having a "meeting," complete with secret signals, passwords, and so on. Violet and I even stood on stacked boxes and orange crates to peer in the window, but we could see and hear nothing and we drew the attention of the "guard," who chased us away. Young as I was, I never once dreamed of entering without Charles's permission. After all, he was the club's president, and his commands were obeyed without question.

One bright and sunny afternoon, Charles came to tell Violet and me we could go in, but only if we pulled on the rope hanging over the doorway. At last! This was our opportunity to see what treasures they must have stored away, what mysterious rituals were going on in there. Violet, several years older than me, must have smelled a rat, for she hung back, all the time pushing *me* forward. My four-year-old mind never questioned what my brother was telling me, so I walked up boldly, yanked on the rope, and proceeded to go in.

Charles grabbed my arm. "Wait a minute," he said. "You have to pull harder than that! And you have to stand right here," he scolded, as he pushed me into the proper spot. I didn't even notice the smirks and winks on the other boys' faces. Taking a deep breath, I gave the rope a mighty jerk. Attached to the rope's end, but set far enough back from the roof's edge so it couldn't be seen from ground zero, was a tin can filled with rocks and water—all of which tumbled down on my uplifted face. Unfortunately, the can's lid was still attached, just bent outward, so when this contraption fell I not only got wet, but got a deep gash in my forehead from the can lid.

Charles streaked toward the house yelling for Mother (I think this was his first "track event"), while Stanley and Cecil could only wring their hands in horror at the sight of the blood streaming down their sister's face. Violet split for home, as did the other neighborhood boys. Mother and Charles ran out to lead me into the house, as there was so much blood I couldn't have found my own way. I must say Mother handled the situation very calmly, keeping her wits about her as she sent Charles running to the drugstore for sterile bandages and adhesive tape, while she began to carefully clean my wound and wash the blood off my face.

After I had been iodined, bandaged, and thoroughly taped around the head, Mother demanded that Charles tell her exactly what had happened. We thought he certainly would be in a lot of trouble, for while the other boys had helped rig up the contraption, it had been his idea.

"Mother, I thought the rocks would hold the can up there, and only water would come down and wet whoever pulled the rope," he tearfully explained. "But she pulled the rope too hard!" (So sorry, guys!)

I guess Mother felt there had been sufficient mayhem and (almost) murder for one day, and that Charles had been sufficiently punished by seeing what harm he'd caused to his sister, for his expected spanking never materialized. I, however, still bear a scar on my hairline that serves as a reminder of how gullible I was. It was a hard way to learn that when something sounds too good to be true, it usually is! The experience also reinforced Daddy's oft-stated belief that girls shouldn't join in boys' games, as things might get a bit rough.

On Pearl Street when it rained, we played in what was jokingly called the "parlor," for it was a seldom-used room. A pattern of large circles on the rug was perfect for the boys' endless games of marbles. Of course this was considered a boys' game, so Leah and I were forced to watch from the sidelines. Charles had the largest collection of marbles, for he played against most of the neighborhood boys, and with his excellent aim and strong young fingers, he was often the winner—so much so that they quite often were reluctant to play with him. Stanley and Cecil, however, were always ready for a game.

Mother overheard Charles accuse Cecil of taking his favorite "shooter," which Cecil vehemently denied. Charles was becoming quite angry until Cecil, with a look of total yet intense innocence on his face, loudly proclaimed, "Naw, Chas, I wouldn't have it, 'cause I didn't got it!" Unable to restrain herself, Mother went into peals of laughter over this fractured English, and even Charles had to laugh. The tension was broken, which was a good thing because our parents tolerated no fighting among us.

It was on Pearl Street that I was going to start kindergarten in September at Lincoln Elementary, even though I wouldn't be five until December. I would be a "big kid" like my brothers, for they were all in school. I enjoyed hearing them tell what they had learned, who their favorite teachers were, and which one was the prettiest—usually a tie between Ms. Miller, Ms. Neu, and Ms. Steele. Mother said I had been picking out words from the newspaper for quite some time, so I must have really been paying attention to their discourses. I was excited at the prospect of learning to read. Perhaps I sensed, even then, what a vital role reading would play in my life. I could scarcely wait to get started.

Railroad Crossing

One sunny afternoon in that summer before I started kindergarten, Leah and I were sitting on the back steps cracking black walnuts and eating their delectable meat. The shells of these nuts are very hard, so we had to use a hammer to open them. At least, I hammered, and Leah ate. Mother came out of the house and walked by us, saying only she'd be "right back." After a bit, when we began to have our fill of nuts, it seemed awfully quiet around there, and Leah began to cry, "I want my mommy!"

"Don't cry, Leah, we'll find her," I assured her. But where could she be? We knew she wasn't in the house; it was much too silent, with no sounds of either cleaning or cooking emanating from it.

The bright idea occurred to me that she must have gone over to Grandmother's, and from that thought it was only a step to decide we'd surprise her by "finding" her. We started down the alley.

I don't know why I decided to take the shortcut across the railroad tracks instead of our usual route down to the Tenth Street crossing, where a guard sat in his little shack, raising and lowering black-and-white striped gates to let cars and people go across safely. So, off we went, across the switching yards and past the roundhouse.

Leah was still a toddler, and only now beginning to walk well. She was so young and small that she had to put one leg over each railroad track, sit on its top, then swing the other leg over while I helped her keep her balance. There must have been twenty to thirty sets of tracks to cross, or at least it seemed so, not counting the first few sets of railroad tracks where passenger and fast freight trains raced along the right-of-way, heading for New York and points east. I had unwittingly picked the apex of the switching yards to make our crossing.

Almost three-quarters of the way across we looked up to see Uncle Horace, Grandma's half-brother, approaching us from the opposite direction and heading toward the railroad station. "Hey, where you kids going?" he queried. We looked a mess, I'm sure, for we were tired and dirty, and crying had left smeared streaks on our faces. "Oh, we're just going over to Grandma's house to meet Mother," we replied, a lot more confidently than we actually felt. It had never seemed such a long way to go when Mother was with us, and she had always carried Leah; it was not much of a shortcut after all. Uncle Horace kept on his way, while we continued our laborious journey.

We finally got across the tracks, but then I wasn't sure which direction to take. I saw a lady in her yard watering flowers and asked her if she knew where Mrs. Morgan's house was. She looked at us thoughtfully for a moment, as though wondering what two such young children were doing out there all alone, but finally she said, "Go on down this street a block that way," pointing west, "and then go down for two more."

As we neared our destination, I recognized the area. Thank goodness! When we walked up onto the front porch, Grandma was at home, and very glad yet surprised to see us. "Where's your mother?" Grandma asked, and my heart sank because that must mean she wasn't there. Grandmother gave her bedraggled grandchildren a quick hug, a cookie, and a glass of milk, which we were almost too tired to drink; then she gave us a quick bath and popped us into bed for a nap.

In the meantime Mother had returned home only to find her two daughters missing. Frantic, she ran down to Tenth Street and asked the crossing guard if he had seen us come that way, because it was surely the direction we would have taken if we were going to cross the tracks at all. She never imagined we would have crossed the tracks in the place we actually did. Of course he hadn't seen us, because we simply hadn't gone that way. Oh, there wasn't any rule against it, for it had never occurred to either parent we would ever do such a thing; therefore, we had never been told not to!

Mother, by now quite frantic and almost out of her wits, ran to use a neighbor's phone to call Grandma. I don't know what sort of punishment Grandmother was meting out that day or what lesson she was trying to teach Mother, but she said, "No, they're not here." How Mother finally found out where we were I never discovered, but the next thing Leah and I knew she was running up the stairs to us crying, hair disheveled, arms outstretched as she hugged us close and kissed us before exacting our solemn promise to never again do such a thing!

When we got back home Daddy was in the bathroom shaving, apparently quite calm, but I could tell he was furious because his lips were curling and quivering. His anger was directed first at Mother for leaving us alone, and second toward Uncle Horace for not staying to help us the rest of the way and make sure we were safe, when it was obvious there was no adult in attendance. Daddy shuddered at the thought that a fast passenger train, or even a slow freight, could have come by at any time while we were negotiating those tracks. Relative or no, Daddy couldn't understand *any* adult not stopping to help two little ones who were so obviously in danger. It took him a while to forgive Mother, but he never, as long as he lived, ever forgave Uncle Horace.

Mother tried to explain that she had only gone a couple of doors away to a neighbor's, to show her some of the school dresses she was making for me. She thought we had seen the direction in which she went, and certainly if we had crossed the railroad tracks at the right place, our path would have taken us right by the neighbor's house and Mother would have seen us.

We had to be especially good for what seemed like a long time, and we didn't want Mother out of our sight for even a minute. While we didn't get a spanking for this escapade, our transgression was indelibly printed on my mind because for the first time in our young lives, Mother told us that if we couldn't be good she would put us *all* in an orphanage. I hadn't known that one could get rid of one's children by giving them away.

Parade

Every Fourth of July, Elkhart erupted in celebration of the occasion. For a long time I thought it was a party for my brother Cecil, since that date was his birthday. The high point of the day, before the fireworks that started at dusk, was a *gigantic* parade. People put on costumes, people whom you never would have dreamed during the rest of the year would want to dress up and perform in an event like this, both adults and children. The parade route ran the entire length of Main Street, from the main post office all the way down to the railroad tracks and the train depot, before disbanding.

Everywhere there were balloons, flags, ribbons, bunting, and anything else the city thought would add to the festival air. Booths lined both sides of the street, and vendors did a brisk business selling cotton candy, popcorn, hot dogs, and soft drinks. Nothing in our young lives ever tasted as good as that hot buttered popcorn, washed down with ice-cold lemonade, on a warm summer day. We weren't allowed to eat hot dogs since they contained pork, which for us was against our religion, but their smell on the breeze surely made our mouths water.

One family dressed up like jugglers and tossed their pins in the air with total abandon. Several bands wearing jaunty uniforms played rousing Sousa marches that made everyone's feet tap to the beat of their drummer, while majorettes pointed their high-stepping toes and twirlers tossed batons effortlessly skyward. Crowds lined the sidewalks on both sides of Main Street, yelling, calling out, encouraging, and applauding the various parade participants.

Mother had made Charles a clown costume, covering his face with grease paint while we all, in fascination, stood around in the kitchen and watched his transformation. Authentic in every detail, he looked as though he'd just left Ringling Brothers Circus to do a little sideshow. His act consisted of turning somersaults and handsprings along the parade route. Physically gifted and athletic as he was, he never slackened his pace or rested during his performance, but he *did* work up a sweat. The crowds went wild over this acrobatic youngster who was so obviously giving his all. Charles was only around eight years old at the time, small-statured but wiry, and so obviously supremely capable of doing what he did. The grin on his face wasn't entirely his makeup, either, but a total enjoyment of being out in front, in the limelight. That ease and enjoyment of performing lasted throughout his life.

I too was in the parade. For me, Mother had made a costume of turquoise crepe paper cut into long strips, rather like a hula skirt. Leis were strung around my neck, and I wore a gold paper crown. I walked until my young legs got tired, then climbed into a very long wagon whose canopy was decorated with turquoise streamers. It was pulled along by Brownie, a relative's well-behaved german shepherd, and guided by my brothers, Cecil and Stanley. Brownie too had a few leis festooned around his neck. Instead of merely resting, I curled up and fell asleep in front of everyone. Ever resourceful, Mother grabbed a pen from her purse, quickly made a sign, and attached it prominently to the wagon, announcing that I was "Sleeping Beauty." This elicited quite a bit of laughter and amusement from the crowd. I slept on, waking only when the parade was over to discover I had won first prize in my age group.

Quite naturally, Charles also won a prize. Who could resist rewarding that little boy who had cartwheeled his way down the length of Main Street and right into the hearts of the onlookers? When Charles stepped forward to receive his prize, some of the grease paint had come off his face as a result of the sweat he had worked up. The judges did a double take: "Oh, is that a little *colored* boy?" They conferred hastily and nervously among themselves.

Mother walked over to the judges. She said something sharply to them, exactly what I don't know, and pointed to the crowd, which was enthusiastically cheering at the announcement that Charles Gordon had won first place overall and first place in his age group. The judges quickly decided to give the prize to him anyway.

But Charles never forgot those looks of consternation and their momentary hesitation, nor the fact that they would have denied him his well-deserved prize simply because of the color of his skin. After all, as he later pointed out, he was not the red-white-black colors of his greasepaint, either; if one had been so easily and readily accepted, why not the other? This was among Charles's first experiences of the "white mask, black world" phenomenon.

Mother used this occurrence to expound on what would become over the years her oft-repeated theory that you must not only *do* your best, you must *be* the best; the world would then have to acknowledge your accomplishments for what they really were. None of us kids had stopped to think about what race we belonged to, except that we were members of the human race. It was a new lesson to us. We determined that henceforth we *would* be the best, and the world would have to recognize our excellence.

Young as he was, her words seemed to light a fire of determination in Charles that never left him. Even though the world might consider him black, as had the parade officials, by being the best he would still be the winner.

7

Lafayette Street

Radio Days and a Fire

We had to create our own entertainment, for television was as yet unheard-of, our old Victrola was more "canned sound" than musical, and even radio was still a novelty. It was a real treat to gather around the radio as a family to listen to specific programs; there was no idle "just having the radio on" without a specific program in mind. We each had our favorites. Mother was a fan of some of the first "soaps": *One Man's Family, Ma Perkins,* and *The Life of Mary Marlin,* which she frequently tuned into while ironing, and her tears sprayed the clothes almost as often as did the sprinkler bottle.

Daddy was an avid listener to one M. J. DeHaan, who, if I remember correctly, preached on Sunday morning against the religion Mother was pursuing; this caused no end of arguments between them. Daddy considered listening to this radio program his "going to church" time. He argued that he didn't need to go to a church edifice to worship, particularly since he would have had to go to one of the two black churches in town—heaven forbid. He claimed to be a better Christian than most of the people who attended the Baptist or Methodist churches, both located on the South Side. I've often wondered just how he knew who were sinners over there and who were not if he never attended.

Daddy liked *Lum and Abner*, followed by *Gabriel Heater and His Up-to-the-Minute News*, while on Sunday afternoons we all enjoyed *Major Bowes and His Amateur Hour*, *The Shadow*, and then *Amos 'n' Andy* (which Daddy said he enjoyed because he knew colored people who talked and acted just like them). Then there was *Edgar Bergen and Charlie McCarthy*, and of course, the inimitable *Jack Benny Program*.

We were sparing in our use of electricity; therefore, we all listened to the same programs at the same time. The one exception was when Daddy would let me listen to a Sunday evening program, *The Voice of Firestone*, for he knew I especially enjoyed the classics, both light and heavy. I was also a fanatical fan of two colored groups: a choir, Wings Over Jordan, and a quartet called the Southernaires, both of which had shows that were aired on Sunday morning, usually at the same time we had breakfast. It was the single most peaceful meal of the week, primarily because I was in the other room, ears glued to the radio, and unable to hear if there was any fussing or arguing going on.

We children enjoyed afternoons spent listening to *Little Orphan Annie* and then *Jack Armstrong, the All-American Boy!* Mother would turn the radio on for us—an operation we were not permitted to perform—after which she proceeded to read the newspaper while we became engrossed in the adventures of Annie and Jack.

One day we were so deeply absorbed in these programs that at first none of us heard the bells and alarms of the fire truck. But then they sounded very close, so we rushed to the window to see what was going on, with Charles first in line as usual. We saw firemen coming out of the house next door carrying a blanket-covered stretcher; a few wisps of smoke still emanated from a broken kitchen window. Mother jumped up from her chair, threw down the newspaper, and ran outside, after admonishing us to stay inside right where we were.

We knew there were two brothers who lived in that house. The older brother worked and took care of Fred, who was mentally retarded. Fred was a familiar sight around the neighborhood because he often mowed people's grass or chopped wood to earn a bit of money. The only dialogue we'd ever had with him consisted of "Hi, Fred" or "Bye, Fred." Daddy said Fred had more "get-up-and-go" than a lot of people who seemed normal, but we kids were forbidden to carry on a conversation with him.

Charles stood at the window and reported that Mother was talking to several of the firemen. He said she was twisting her hands as if she were in pain, which scared us because she was usually quite calm. Charles then told us he could see a stretcher with someone on it, but since it was fully covered he couldn't tell who was on it before they drove away. At that point Mother began heading back into the house, so Charles scrambled down from the window, afraid she would know he'd been watching.

"You kids were listening to that radio, and because you were so wrapped up in those programs, poor Fred died! Burned to death! You didn't even hear his cries for help!" Mother shrieked at us. Stunned, we could only hang our heads and listen. It seemed Fred had tried to build a fire in the wood-burning kitchen stove, and experiencing some difficulty in getting it started, he decided to pour kerosene on it. Blazing up, it set fire to his hair and clothing. Not knowing what to do and likely in a panic, he evidently tried to smother the flames by wrapping himself in the kitchen curtains, and they too caught fire. By the time the fire department arrived it was already too late; we never found out who first saw the fire and reported it. I do know it hadn't been us, even though we were in the house closest to him.

We bore the guilt and felt responsible for Fred's death for a long time. If Mother said it was our fault, it must have been. But never again did we gather around the radio to listen to the adventures of Annie and Jack. Neither did we ever ask Mother why *she* hadn't heard Fred's screams herself, since she was in the same room with us and closer to the door.

Fred's brother (we never knew his name) moved shortly after that. The house was sold, and a new family moved in. They installed a furnace and a gas stove, but for years afterward on the rare evenings when Mother and Daddy were out and we were home alone, we could still hear the thump of wood being chopped in the basement next door, just like Fred used to do. Stranger still, we never heard this sound when our parents were there. Several times I had nightmares in which I unlocked our basement door and called out into the darkness, "Who's there?" only to feel a rush of air as a dark shape whooshed past me. Frightened, I always made sure the basement door was locked tight if our parents were away, so that nothing could "get" me and I would be safe.

Now I know that those evening trips of my parents involved their going to South Bend, Indiana, so Daddy could get a haircut, for none of the white barbershops in Elkhart would cut colored people's hair. Mother bought a home barbershop kit so she could trim the boys' hair. I thought she did this because she was so smart and knew how to save money, but Daddy never entrusted her with *his* locks. I thought this rather picky of him, for the boys' cuts always looked great to me. And I heard Mother state on more than one occasion that "there's only two weeks' difference between a good and a bad haircut."

Religion

Doing what Mother and Daddy told us often defied our childish comprehension, but to dare otherwise meant risking the loss of their love—with its attendant threat, both implied and stated, of abandonment. We felt their presence was the only thing standing between us and a black sea of aloneness. Since Mother was never wrong, we thought she must be God, and her punishments were certainly swift and sure. What confused us even more was that Daddy's words also had to be considered, even above hers: did that make him God too? And his punishments were just as swift and sure as hers! From an early age we had to accept that this was how things were; the only alternative, disobedience, would have meant our total abandonment, which is the deepest-seated fear of any child. Our unspoken compromise was found in the words of an old hymn: "Trust and obey, for there's no other way . . ."

Mornings for us began with kneeling prayers, and woe betide us if we neglected to say them yet again at bedtime. Thanks were to be offered before each meal, but since Daddy always asked the blessing, all we had to do was fold our hands and bow our heads.

Friday afternoons were spent taking our weekly baths in preparation for the start of the Sabbath, which lasted from sunset Friday to sunset Saturday. We gathered with Mother (Daddy didn't observe this practice at that time) and sang appropriate hymns to welcome in the Sabbath, followed by a prayer or appropriate Bible verse from each of us. After that, we could sit around and read our Bibles or study our Sabbath school lesson (which also had to be done on a daily basis) until bedtime, knowing that in the morning it would be kneeling prayers and hymn-singing again before breakfast, and then a walk in our clean Sabbath finery down dusty, unpaved Wagner Avenue, past the railroad roundhouse—where hopefully we could avoid getting a misty faceful of soot from the engines that were being worked on—as we headed for the small colored church just a block past Grandma's house. I'm sure we presented quite a picture: Mother surrounded by her five children decked out in their "Sunday" best (on Saturday!), the three boys walking slightly ahead and Leah and I on either side of Mother, white shoes immaculately polished, hair crimped and curled, dresses starched and ruffled. We didn't have to worry about cars going by because none of the colored people in that part of town *had* cars, and whites didn't drive on that street.

Usually we popped in at Grandma's for a quick visit before continuing on to church, for Mother was insistent we be present and in our seats before the 9:30 a.m. starting time. It was impressed on us at an early age to be on time. After Sabbath school ended there was a fifteen-minute Home Missionary program, followed by the main preaching service at 11:00. Unless we had a guest speaker, church was usually out by 12:30 or 1:00 p.m., and after another short visit at Grandma's, we'd head for home and dinner. Mother cooked our Sabbath dinner on Friday to be reheated the next day, because we were not supposed to do any work on the Sabbath, which included cooking. We were not allowed to do anything frivolous or entertaining on that day. We returned to church for the Young People's Meeting at 3:30, and at sunset we had Vesper services, for which we sang and prayed before "closing" the Sabbath.

We could not go to the movies, dance, or attend school-sponsored sports events if they were held during our Sabbath hours. No jewelry except a wristwatch could be worn, not even a wedding ring. No makeup was permitted, nor could the women wear jeans or slacks. We were also vegetarians; meat was a rarity on the Gordon table, appearing only at Thanksgiving and Christmas, when we had turkey. In my mid-teen years Mother would occasionally fry a chicken, but pork was absolutely forbidden. (Don't ask me how I ate that nickel's worth of bologna from Mr. Davidson's store; it never occurred to me that it contained pork!)

Mother had taken up this religion when Charles was around five or six years old. It was no wonder that in later years he often made it a point to brag about suffering from "housemaid's knee" by the time he was seven as a result of being forced to kneel to pray so often! In addition, by the time I was ten, I had to play the piano for the hymn singing both at home and at church—for *all* the services. By the time I was seventeen and graduating from high school, I was suffering "hymnal burnout," for Mother wouldn't let me refuse to play.

For the first several years of Mother's intense involvement in what I now believe was a cult-type religion, and before she founded an all-colored church, we attended the First Church in Elkhart with an all-white congregation. I enjoyed the music, but Charles had a habit that really annoyed Mother, that of dozing off during the sermons and awakening only when Mother jabbed him in the side.

The First Church had a school held in a one-room classroom that served only the children of members. Mother enrolled my brothers, but I wasn't yet old enough to attend. The boys walked the three miles or so between our house and the school, although Cecil was extremely skittish about having to pass an old cemetery not far from their destination. He confessed he was afraid of seeing ghosts.

Mother pooh-poohed this, saying, "Oh, Cecil, there's no such thing as a ghost, but if there *is*, God will protect you!"

"Maybe so, Mother, but he's way up there in heaven, and these ghosts are right down here!" Cecil fairly stammered in his sincerity. He had a modicum of belief in what Mother told him but would invariably cross the street *before* he got to Grace Lawn Cemetery, rejoining his brothers only after they had safely passed by. Today he is buried in that cemetery, the only one of us buried next to Mother and Daddy. It was sixty years before he got there, but I've sometimes wondered if he had a premonition that it would be his final resting place, and if he in turn would try to become a "ghost" to scare any other unwary kids who might walk by.

Attendance at that church school came to an abrupt end when several of the older girls were caught dancing nude in the furnace room, putting on a show for some of the older boys. A small portable radio provided music, and they were dancing "lasciviously," as one church elder described it—whirling, turning, keeping in rhythm with the music's beat, with no tops or bottoms on and no shoes. Unfortunately, some of the younger boys heard the music, followed the sound, and witnessed the spectacle. These younger boys couldn't resist telling their parents, so the jig was up. The parents seemed most horrified by the fact that the girls were *dancing,* which was expressly forbidden, but only slightly less so by their nudity.

Mother, however, was appalled: nakedness *and* dancing in a church school? Was this what she was paying tuition for? Where was the teacher who was supposed to be watching over these young lambs? Out to lunch, perhaps? Mother decided that maybe public school wouldn't be such a bad idea after all; at least the children would be more closely supervised. The boys were quickly enrolled in Lincoln Elementary School, just two short blocks from home. Cecil loved it because he didn't have to pass one single cemetery.

Being educated in this cult-type religion from such tender years, we believed we were unworthy, that we were all sinners with no hope of redemption, and that hellfire and damnation was our destination even in the face of repentance, which placed an additional burden on us as children. It caused a tremendous amount of stress, so much so that for years we believed we were not worthy of love, respect, or happiness. We lived forever on the cutting edge between heaven and hell. It was not enough that we were different from our friends and classmates by being colored; we were definitely set apart from the world's mainstream.

This difference preyed on our young minds as nothing else possibly could have. We simply wanted to be like other kids and, by transference, the same as those people who populated our world. This was totally denied us, and it was only after years of effort on our own parts that we discovered these beliefs to be in error. It certainly haunted Charles almost to the end of his life, until he found through his years with Susan, the cowboys, and Native Americans, that these things were simply not so. We were as worthy to accept those responses from people's hearts as anyone else.

THE COWBOY'S CHURCH

Down a valley I rode my horse one fine day,
And the sights that I saw made me want to pray.

Now, I'm not a reg'lar church-goin' man,
Just try to treat people as fair as I can.

With all of this beauty in one single place
It seemed I was lookin' God right in the face.

The mornin' was chill, and the sun was just up.
I had knelt by a stream, used my hat for a cup.

Far off in the distance the mountains rose high,
Like a rocky cathedral a-reachin' for sky.

Midway from the top there were ledges of trees,
Further down there was flowers, and sweet honey bees.

Them bees was plumb crazy, and scoutin' each flower,
As the sun rose and warmed them, hour by hour.

There was sage brush and piñon and cottonwood trees;
Angel eyes can't find nothin' prettier than these.

A red-winged blackbird flashed bright in the sky,
While eagles squawked loudly their "out-huntin'" cry.

Through close-growin' piñon I thought I saw bear
But he turned and walked off like nobody was there.

A fish or two jumped high in the river's bed,
And sunlight sparked them in gray, gold, and red.

A deer passed right by me and drank from the stream,
A doe, moving slowly, as though in a dream.

I heard a jackrabbit slip under some brush,
And mostly all 'round me was this great big hush.

It seemed like this place was a corner of land
Personally laid out by God's very own hand.

All around me was nature unspoiled and clean;
Only man, with his mind, could be tortured and mean.

On that day I promised that I'd always do
Only what God and Nature wanted me to.

I worshipped in silence, and now I can see
Love of God and of Nature made a man out of me!

Shirley Gordon Jackson

A COWBOY'S RELIGION

These lands are our churches,
The rivers and streams running through,
Our holy water.
These rocks and hills are sacred temples,

While vaulted skies shape the ceilings
Of our cathedrals.
Our carillons are the piercing cry
Of eagle, the lowing of cattle,
A restless movement of horses,
In a coyote's lonely howl,
Becoming our hymns as they are
Carried on breezes that move
Over and beyond this place
Until, at last, they come to rest
In whispered benedictions of the heart.

Shirley Gordon Jackson

Trees

Perhaps one of the reasons I loved Elkhart's trees so much is because when I was about ten I had a love affair with one. A tall maple stood in our front yard between the sidewalk and the street. In winter it was bare, but in the spring and summer it leafed out into a shady green umbrella that helped cool the yard and the house. In the fall it made a display of colors: red, orange, and yellow. How I loved that tree! Straight-trunked, its rough bark always felt alive under my young fingers.

After having read hundreds of fairy tales I had become an imaginative, incurable romantic at a very tender age, and nothing suited me better than to pretend I was greatly loved, tenderly hugged, and fondly caressed. In one of my play-acting spells, that tree became symbolic of the lover I was much too young to have in real life. It wasn't a sexual love, although I probably got a textural, sensuous feeling when I touched or kissed its bark; it was more a feeling of strength that flowed between us, a strength I felt I could lean upon.

One hot summer day I took a long chiffon scarf, wrapped it twice around my waist, then tied the other end around the tree. I leaned back so that the scarf, which I pretended was my lover's arms, supported my weight. I imagined that the tree was telling me it loved me, it would be strong for me, and would keep me safe from harm. So I kissed the rough bark, which to my imagination must have simulated a man's unshaven face with a beard, and immediately it became a lover's face touching mine. Oh, I thought, to have someone strong to hold me, to care for me! I kissed the tree repeatedly.

Suddenly, I heard loud laughter. I looked up to see Charles herding Mother, Leah, Cecil, and Stanley to front-row, center-aisle places on the steps of the front porch, pointing toward me, watching their sister doing a dumb thing like kissing a tree. And Cecil's laughter was particularly raucous.

I think Mother realized this play-acting was a subconscious desire for affection, of needing to feel there was something or someone stronger than me who would shelter and protect me. Although he laughed, I think Charles also, at least later in life, recognized that I was expressing an intense hunger and desire for love, affection, and security. Ever the showman, he couldn't resist the opportunity to direct, while I was cast in the unsuspecting role of star.

This was the last time I ever performed that little play, for by having been observed it lost its magic. It was too private an affair to share with or even try to explain to anyone, and in any event I doubt I would have been able to find words to explain my actions. But hidden away in a recess of my young mind I had already developed an intuition that the sheltering and the strength weren't going to come from my parents or family.

But from whence were these deep longings coming? I was, I believe, sensing undercurrents of dissatisfaction between my parents that were beginning to shake my fundamental belief that the family was all; I was realizing that they might not always be there for me. Fractures were appearing here and there, and it seemed only a matter of time before the pieces broke. I didn't know if we could survive the inner forces that were working their way to the surface, and I didn't want to believe there could possibly be a breakdown of my family unit. My parents were supposed to love each other and, by extension, us. Yet other messages were filtering through, and all I could do was turn a deaf ear to them. Not hearing or admitting to them allowed me to ignore them, to bury them deep in my subconscious mind. What I neither saw nor heard could not possibly exist. To admit otherwise would have given credence to my suspicions, and I was not ready to hear anything about that.

This was my first early experience in denying what promised to become a reality.

"Me Jane, You Tarzan"

Spring always came to Indiana suddenly. One day the ground would be covered with snow, cold winds blasting into the air, while plant life seemed dead. Then one morning you would wake up to a soft, sweet-smelling air, and miraculously, tiny buds and leaves would open up on tree and bush alike. Almost overnight the lilac bushes in our front yard seemed to burst into bloom, perfuming the whole neighborhood with their heady fragrance.

After dreary winter months spent struggling in and out of snowsuits and galoshes, on spring days like this the first thing we kids wanted to do was go barefoot, but our parents were dead set against this. Their explanation: "Anyone seeing you would think you were little niggers who didn't *have* no shoes!" This puzzled me, because a family of twenty-two children living across the street had been running up and down barefoot for at least a week. I could understand twenty-two children not having enough shoes to go around, but there were only five of us: how could anyone possibly misconstrue our newfound spring freedom? But this was a *rule,* and for breaking it I suffered the consequences.

This particular day, with sunshine pouring out of an azure sky and soft breezes wafting here and there, Mother decided to go downtown on some errands while Daddy was home on his lunch break. Nodding in his rocking chair, it never occurred to him that his usually obedient daughter Shirley, intoxicated by the smell of spring in the air, would not only remove her shoes but climb the tree in our side yard. The bark of the tree seemed to come alive under my bare feet, making it easy to gain purchase, and I, who was *not* a tomboy, who *never* did anything this disobedient, blithely reached the lower branches of the tree and rested there, a princess surveying my leafy domain. How different the world looked from higher up!

Finally my conscience smote me, and I thought the better part of valor would be to descend before I got found out. That's when I discovered it was much more difficult to get down than it had been to climb up. Reaching a lower limb, I decided it wouldn't hurt me to jump that short distance, since the ground was thickly padded with a fresh crop of tall weeds, which would certainly cushion my landing. So I jumped.

What I couldn't see through the weeds was a piece of wood, a two-by-four about a foot in length, with an extremely long rusty nail sticking straight up through it. (This was later determined to have been overlooked by Cecil while working on one of his innumerable "constructions," in this case a see-saw that never worked properly, like all his other efforts at building things.) I landed squarely on that nail and it pierced my left foot. At first, it didn't even hurt. I thought I had simply stepped on a cinder, a stone, or something of that nature; I tried to brush it off, but it wouldn't budge. Looking down I saw that board with the nail still *in* my foot, and I screamed for my brothers. They must have heard the terror in my voice, for that was one time I remember calling and getting an instant response from them. They flew around the corner of the house to where I had fallen to the ground.

Charles held me under my arms while Cecil and Stanley each grabbed hold of that board and, bracing themselves, pulled the nail out. Then Charles tenderly picked me up and carried me into the house, up the back steps and through the kitchen and the dining room, where Daddy jumped up to take control. "Take her into the bathroom," he ordered, and Charles, still holding me as if I might break, deposited me on the lid of the commode.

Daddy put an enameled basin under my foot and started pouring warm water with a *lot* of Lysol in it onto my wound, over and over, while the blood flowed freely. The boys, Charles in front, crowded into the doorway of the small bathroom, and I could see tears running down Charles's cheeks. Patting my shoulder awkwardly, he kept saying, like a mantra, "It's gonna be okay, Shirley, it's gonna be okay."

Just then Mother came up the alley and through the back door, where she saw a trail of blood leading up the steps and through the kitchen and the dining room. I'm sure the sight scared her half out of her wits, not knowing how severely injured one of her children might be.

Daddy carefully dried my foot with a clean towel, asking Mother for a piece of old sheeting to use as a bandage. He put something on the wound called "Sano Black Salve," which besides being quite odoriferous was also guaranteed to cure pneumonia, rheumatism, ringworm, and a host of other ailments. He wrapped my foot snugly, then carried me gently to the living-room sofa. He told the boys they could go back outside and play, since Mother was now there to take care of me. For the first time that I could remember he was a bit late returning to work from lunch, but he evidently wasn't leaving without feeling sure I was okay.

Neither of my parents seemed concerned about the possibility of tetanus because of the salve Daddy had used. It must have been some powerful stuff, because after that first afternoon when I felt some throbbing pains, my foot proceeded to heal nicely and I never came down with "lockjaw." (Charles jokingly said that it might not have been a bad idea to stop my chattering so much, but I could sense his gladness over my uneventful recovery.)

Mother suggested I try to take a nap, and by now I was rather exhausted from all the excitement. Before I drifted off to sleep, she stood beside me where I rested on the sofa and berated me in no uncertain terms, "This is what happens to little girls who disobey their parents; you knew you weren't supposed to go barefoot and you see what happened? Remember, your sins will always find you out!" I could only nod my head weakly in assent, for after all, hadn't Mother-God spoken?

Mother then went out the front door, going down the street to visit with a neighbor, which I felt was rather cold-hearted of her. How did she know I would be all right? I knew better than to ask.

That, of course, was the end of my childhood "barefoot" days, although I still wistfully watched all those kids across the street as they cavorted all over the place—in the dirt, in the weeds—not stubbing a toe on the cement sidewalk, never getting so much as a cut or scratch on their feet!

In later life I absolutely reveled in kicking my shoes off as soon as I entered the house, but never again did I feel free to walk barefoot in the great outdoors. My tree-climbing days were definitely ended.

Family Ties

With all of us intensely involved in school and church activities, time sped by. Charles could abide only so much sitting or inactivity before his energies hollered for release. He was therefore producer and director for whatever energetic physical actions he thought he and his brothers should be doing: collecting glass and tin cans for the "Old Rags and Bottles" man so they could buy penny candy, or making "zap guns" from blocks of wood, clothespins, and rubber bands sliced from old tire inner tubes, after which they would conduct battles in which Charles would be the "good cowboy" while they were the "cattle rustlers." It was Cecil, anxious for each brother to have his own zap gun, who rummaged in the garage for an old inner tube and cut up one he successfully found there—only to discover later it was not old, but a new one Daddy kept for a spare. Cecil got a spanking for not having checked it out beforehand, but he didn't rat on Charles, who had told him to slice it up.

It was Charles who egged Stanley and Cecil on: follow the iceman's wagon in the hot summertime, snatch a large chunk of chipped ice when the driver went into a house to make a delivery, wrap this in a piece of brown paper bag and share it with the rest of us. Make stilts from scrap lumber for all three of them, even though Charles was the only one who could actually walk on them: Stanley and Cecil always fell off. It was also his idea to show Stanley and Cecil how to smash the bottoms of their shoes into the side of a tin can so they fit snugly, to make a sound like horses galloping when they "clopped" over the ground. In this manner one of them could be the Lone Ranger's sidekick, Tonto, or Gene Autry's buddy, Pat Buttram—while Charles had to be, and always was, the star of whatever drama they were acting out.

Charles once sneaked out of our grandparents' house with one of Grandpa's Stetson hats so he could be authentically dressed for a game of cowboys and Indians. He continued to wear that Stetson everywhere—except over to Grandpa's—and Grandpa never knew he was missing one of his numerous pieces of Western headgear. Actually, I have a suspicion Grandpa *did* know, and enjoyed Charles's love for all things Western, for he too had that affinity. That was why he used to tell Charles stories of a legendary cowboy named Stackerlee. Charles even spurred Daddy on to tell us of some of the cowboy movies he had seen, especially those starring Tom Mix—at the dinner table, no less!

Behind the garage, out of sight from the kitchen window, Charles took dried corn silks, rolled them inside strips of brown paper, and twisted the ends to make a crude "cigarette," which he generously shared with his brothers. Unfortunately, Cecil got sick after doing this, so that experiment was ended, for Mother got the story out of Cecil and punishment was twofold for that episode: they had broken two of her cardinal rules, playing with matches and *smoking!*

Playing kick-the-can helps develop your leg muscles and eye coordination, Charles swore—something that never would have occurred to the rest of us—thus he always had willing partners to help achieve his goal. It was easy for him to convince his brothers of the rightness of his actions. Charles turned old orange crates, obtained free from the grocery store, into wagons and scooters; he was able to take the wheels off my doll buggy (just the right size for his wagons) in less than sixty seconds, and frequently did! My and Leah's roller skates weren't safe at any time—nailed to the undersides of those scooters, they provided the needed power to operate them. Charles could always "scoot" the fastest. In the summertime, when all this play was in full swing, Mother despaired of keeping the boys in decent shoes, for the concrete sidewalk was very hard on the toe of the shoe used to propel the scooter.

The entire family had bicycles, and it was a familiar sight around Elkhart to see all seven Gordons pedaling madly down the street, with Charles usually in front. He was also first with "Look, Ma, no hands!" and was even able to ride backward while sitting on the handlebars, while we ended up with scratches and bruises in our efforts to follow his lead. After all, if Charles told us we could do something we believed him, not stopping to think that "easy" for that natural athlete might be only painfully accomplished by the rest of us after much trial and error—of which, believe me, there was plenty.

One of his performances we at least had the good sense not to attempt was when he stood on the front porch railing, jumped into the air, and turned a double somersault before landing squarely on his feet. We thought this the most remarkable thing we had ever seen, and he would perform this feat for us whenever we asked him, for as long as we stood there, mouths agape in admiration. Even he knew this wasn't something his brothers could do; then again, perhaps he wanted to have at least one trick in his bag, something only *he* could do, and thereby not always have to share the spotlight. We readily accorded him the title of "The Best."

The boys were so close in age and size that hand-me-downs were the order of the day. Clothing was outgrown long before it began to show signs of wear. Cecil would anxiously eye a particularly attractive sport shirt as it went from Charles to Stanley, then to him. Neither of them seemed to have any sense of deprivation because something was not new; if Charles had worn it, the other two wore it proudly, almost as though it were a badge of honor.

The one item of clothing Daddy didn't believe in handing down was shoes. He said everybody's feet were shaped differently; therefore you "broke in" a new pair in conformation with your own foot pattern, which might be wrong for someone else and thereby lead to a lot of foot trouble in later life. While the boys weren't especially hard on their clothing, in their rough-and-tumble world it seemed Mother was always up on Main Street at the old Boston Store, buying *three* pairs of shoes. (I suspect kick-the-can and the vigorous riding of those homemade wagons and scooters played a large part in this.)

In their early teens, on one such trip Cecil made it well known that he wanted his new shoes to be high-top boots, the kind that reached almost to the knee and had a pouch on the side that came with a jackknife inside, and he persuaded Charles and Stanley to say this was what they too wanted. Looking quite manly in their corduroy knickers and new boots, the boys trooped out of the store in high spirits only to discover there were no knives in the pouches! Mother had unobtrusively removed them.

Cecil pressed for a reason, and Mother said, "I *don't* want to see you boys' initials carved on every tree in town!" Cecil was quite surprised that she had guessed his intentions, but it had been easy to figure out; he loved to whittle and carve on wood, often using good kitchen paring knives and thereby ruining the blades. He could make really neat whistles and small figurines, and I'm sure he had plans to use both Charles's and Stanley's knives in addition to his own. I've often wondered if a woodcarving kit would have been an appropriate gift for Cecil, but money in our household wasn't spent like that.

Very shortly all three lost their enjoyment in those boots, for a lot of time had to be spent lacing them up. Any boy who's ever owned a pair can remember the long laces that went at least halfway up the boot before having to be passed around metal hooks and tied in place. When the next time rolled around for new shoes, they selected the sturdy oxfords and saddle shoes of yore.

For himself, Daddy had his own shoes soled, resoled, then resoled again, and to help them last longer he folded newspaper into a pad and stuffed it inside the shoe over the holes, until he could afford to buy a new pair. But we kids always had the new shoes we needed, when we needed them. I doubt many children's biological fathers would have sacrificed in that manner.

Mother's religious denomination was showing a movie about the dangers of smoking, and the entire family went to see it, including Daddy. How terrible it was to see pictures of people's blackened lungs, to hear their hacking coughs, and to watch them dying painfully of cancer. Daddy was still not a believer in Mother's religion, although he agreed with some of their tenets insofar as healthful living was concerned. But when we returned home, he went to the desk where he kept his private belongings, took out a box of expensive cigars and a new white Meerschaum pipe with its solid gold band, and went to the basement and thrust them all into the furnace, saying he didn't want to set a wrong example in front of us children. He never touched tobacco for the rest of his life, and he lived to be ninety-eight years old.

I do not say this proudly, but the first thing each of us kids did upon leaving home was to purchase a pack of cigarettes and start smoking. So much for example! Or perhaps this was a way of declaring our new independence.

Every summer we had a family reunion in our grandparents' backyard, and anybody who claimed even the remotest kinship (and there were some pretty far-fetched ones) came to enjoy the mounds of food heaped on as many as ten banquet-sized tables, borrowed for the occasion by Daddy from the YWCA where he worked. Everyone brought something, and when those Southern cooks fixed their "company best" dishes, your nose could smell it from blocks away, your mouth watered when you saw it, and when you ate it your stomach thought it had died and gone to heaven.

How tantalizing were the smells of ribs and chicken barbecuing over red-hot coals as hickory smoke floated out over the entire neighborhood. There were huge platters of crisply fried chicken that the Colonel would proudly have called his own; whole hams with a honey glaze that bees felt privileged to have given their very best for; large casseroles of macaroni and cheese, golden and still bubbly on top; mounds of potato salad, both German and American; plus many other kinds of salads, from tossed to jellied, that would suit even the most discriminating of palates. Freshly picked green beans filled several huge bowls; there were homegrown "greens," that Southern staple, with their usual side dishes of golden cornbread, crisp green onions, and sliced tomatoes that had been picked red and ripe that very morning; assorted relishes; olives, both black and green; radishes cut into rose shapes; deviled eggs; and homemade pickles of every kind from sweet to dill. Grandma made dozens of her feather-light rolls, of which there were never enough; fresh pies of apple and berry; and several kinds of cobblers, not to mention the sweet potato and pecan pies! Then, to top it all off, Mother and Grandma both made a freezerful of homemade ice cream.

Mother's religion forbade us to eat anything with pork in it, and a few people did barbecue pork ribs. But there was such a variety of dishes that we didn't mind in the least, nor did we miss it at all: we just overdosed on barbecued chicken, vegetables, and most of all, dessert. Daddy always insisted Mother dish up his plate with only the food she had brought because he didn't trust the other cooks not to put pork in their dishes. Mother told him every year that half the fun was in tasting other people's cooking, but he emphatically said he knew hers had only the best ingredients and he preferred knowing what was in the food he was eating. She could never change his mind on this, either!

Everyone ate until their tummies positively could hold no more, and all anyone could do was sit around in a satisfied stupor. We were ready now for our "program." Grandma's Steinway was moved outside, and I played for everyone to sing all their old favorites. Some people would stand up to say a few words, usually to proclaim that they wouldn't have missed this occasion for anything in the world. I'm sure they told the truth, for no restaurant we knew of offered the variety and tastiness of the foods set out that day.

People would then request a piano solo from me, a vocal solo from Charles, a piece on the violin from Stanley, or even a trio selection with me at the piano, Stanley on his violin, and Leah with her cello. Then the crowd would beg Mother to give a couple of her Paul Laurence Dunbar poems—or readings, as they were popularly called—which she gladly did, for there was nothing she liked better than to be in the spotlight along with her children. I've always sworn she was a frustrated actress, for she was utterly at ease when appearing in public and never had to be asked more than once. Our performances served to make her and Daddy proud of us.

Lincoln Elementary School orchestra and band, 1941; Shirley, *front row, far right* (behind drums). Copyrighted material used by permission of *The Truth.*

Now the party was in full swing, having come to the part we anticipated most: a performance by Charles. None of us knew in advance what that talented brother of ours would do: another song? a dance? tell a story? We knew he could and would take any amusing family incident and imbue it with his own totally theatrical facial and body movements, playing his audience to the hilt and keeping everyone in stitches from beginning to end.

On one of the last occasions that we were all in attendance, during his last year in high school, Charles performed a skit portraying something that had recently happened in the family. It seems Grandfather had come home late one Saturday night from his weekly "night out with the boys" having had one drink too many, so he was not too steady on his feet. Entering the dark house where Grandma was already asleep upstairs, Grandpa found to his dismay she had rearranged the downstairs furniture and he couldn't figure out where he was. Aiming for the bathroom, his tipsy sense of direction got him into the downstairs closet, where he blindly thrashed around, knocking clothes from hangers and swearing like a sailor. Finally, in desperation, he yelled, "Nora! Nora! Come get me outta here!" Grandma, realizing what had happened, was laughing so hard she could scarcely make it downstairs to help him.

In his portrayal, Charles moved and spoke exactly like our drunken grandfather; he even took on Grandma's characteristics when he imitated *her* reactions. You felt you had a ringside seat, watching it all happen right before your eyes. Oh, Grandfather wasn't too happy about his mishap being made public, but even he had to chuckle while Charles brought down the house. It took Grandpa a while to live that one down.

It was my first conscious recognition of Charles's innate star quality and ability to bring characters to life. During the entire performance he still emanated such a sweet and loving spirit that Grandpa couldn't stay—or even really *get*—mad at him.

When Charles entered the fifth grade he wanted to be a patrol boy, a position held by the most popular boys in the school—all of them white, and none of whose parents wanted to include Charles. Their responsibilities were comparable to present-day crossing guards: to help the children cross the street safely. Some of the white parents let the principal know they didn't want a colored boy to be in a position where he could tell their little white children what to do, even though it was for safety's sake.

They didn't know Mother. She could ignore the boys' arguments and minor scraps at school, trusting they could take care of themselves; but you *didn't* refuse to let her kids do something simply because they were colored. To her, that was a non-reason. So to the principal, a Mr. Weldy, she went for a personal conference.

We never knew exactly what she said to him, but shortly afterward Charles was asked to become a patrol boy, an invitation he ecstatically accepted. Our family believed it was the Christian beliefs of the principal that led him to root out discrimination when it was brought to his attention. He and his family were members of the Church of the Brethren, and all became fast friends of our family.

Lincoln Elementary School softball team, circa 1938; Charles, *center, second row from left*. Copyrighted material used by permission of *The Truth*.

Charles felt his responsibilities as a patrol boy quite deeply and took special care of the white belted-and-strapped apparatus made of heavy duck fabric, which was the symbol of his office. His pride even extended to washing it almost daily, until finally Mother had to remonstrate with him: "Look, Charles, you're going to wear that belt out from scrubbing it so much!"

Naturally, when Stanley entered the sixth grade, he was also expected to serve as a patrol boy, the way having been paved by Mother, Charles, and the principal. Stanley, however, didn't have the enthusiasm for it that Charles had had. He was a quiet, gentle boy who preferred to stay in the background, unlike Charles, who reveled in the limelight.

Cecil, too, became a patrol boy, but couldn't keep his grades up enough to stay in the group. It didn't seem to bother him. His enjoyment seemingly came from loudly boasting about his two older brothers, who could do *anything* better than anyone! As time went by, even Leah and I were included as objects of his braggadocio: Leah could play the cello better than anyone; I could play the piano better than anyone.

Charles also played on Lincoln Elementary's softball team, which won the citywide championship three years in a row. Not only did they win those championships; they also had seventeen straight wins over a three-year period, 1936 to 1938. His athletic star was definitely rising.

Good "Sports"

During summer vacations the school district sponsored recreational activities at various elementary school playgrounds around the city. These were the first opportunities we kids had to meet other kids from the more affluent neighborhoods, and to our surprise, they played the same way we did. There were board games, table tennis, jacks, craft projects, baseball and softball, and numerous other sporting events.

At summer's end there was a citywide athletic contest of races and games. My brothers usually took first place in whatever events they entered, either individually or as part of a team. I wasn't much into physical competition, too afraid of getting hurt, but one year I decided to participate in a race and gave it my best while my brothers cheered me on from the sidelines. Imagine my jubilance to find, upon crossing the finish line, that I had won!

Then surprise, surprise: the judges wouldn't give me the ribbon because my brothers had won first place in all *their* events, and they felt it might discourage other children if the Gordon kids won everything. I failed to understand this line of reasoning. If, in a fair race, I had come in first, why shouldn't I get the ribbon so Mother could be proud of me too? After all, it was Mother who had told us to be "the best," and that's what we were trying to accomplish.

That was the first and last time I ever entered a race. I had the distinct feeling that if the Gordons had all been white kids, there would not have been a problem with the awarding of ribbons. This

Charles (age four) and Stanley (age three) playing football in a vacant lot in Elkhart, 1929.

was my own first experience in the "white mask, black world" syndrome Charles would come up against so often. We were not trying to outdo the white kids simply because they were white, for we never considered skin color in our efforts, just tried to be the best in whatever we were doing.

But the colored kids from the South Side never let us forget our own color, with jibes like, "Yeah, you Gordons think you're white, but them judges sure showed you!" They would spit at us, throw dirt on our clothes (out of sight of the adults, of course), and taunt us, "Y'all are still niggers, just like us!" Well, I thought to myself, I may be colored, but I am definitely *not* like you!

One thing was certain: the boys' athletic ability (most particularly that of Charles), combined with our scholastic proclivities and musical talents, helped greatly to open up the minds of quite a few white residents of Elkhart to the fact that colored people could excel in many fields of endeavor. While they weren't ready for social acceptance, they did give us the opportunity to widen both their and our own horizons. Despite the effort of some whites to "keep us in our place," the things we accomplished did cause more than one person to look at our race in a different light, and certainly we made the road easier for others who came along after us.

Images

A tremendous amount of our childhood accomplishments came about at the instigation and insistence of Mother, who, starting with Charles, saw the five of us as her personal "Dream Team." Everything she had ever wanted to do or become was crystallized in her dreams and ambitions for us. We were to be her vindication to the world, and she intended to live, no matter how vicariously, through us. Her recurring theme was "Make me proud of you."

We were pitted not just against other children but against one another from the time we started school. At first it was competition against one another academically. We were never allowed to forget the A or B one of us might have gotten; we soon found that a C or D—or horrors, an F—was just not acceptable. Report card time was not a happy occasion, particularly for Cecil. And when Leah came along Daddy expected her, as the only one of us that he had fathered, to be smarter, more brilliant, and make higher grades than the rest of us. She was an excellent student, but he was never satisfied unless her grades were superior to ours, which put a tremendous amount of pressure on her. Charles and I didn't make it any easier, for our grades were always high; the brunt was borne by Cecil and Stanley.

Cecil was supposed to be a grade ahead of me when he returned from California, where he had lived for a year with Grandmother while she was caring for an ill daughter. Instead, he was put into the second grade with me, which completely devastated him. It was a most unhappy situation and a crushing blow to his ego. If I gave a wrong answer in class it was Cecil who guffawed more loudly than anyone, then reported back to the family that I thought I was so smart. I never told how he was telling other students that I was only his "half-sister." It seemed he wanted to distance himself from me. I knew it was partly because these same students so frequently asked him why he was a different color than I was, which always seemed like a stupid question to me because all five of us had different complexions.

At the end of the school year he had to repeat the second grade while I advanced to third, and his pride was totally undone to feel he'd been "bested" by that half-sister. Mother tried tutoring him at home, but scholastics just wasn't his forte. She let him select a musical instrument to learn to play, but the cornet, the guitar, even drums seemed completely beyond his ability. His disposition, however, was usually so sweet and winning (away from the classroom) that most people overlooked the fact that he was failing in almost every subject.

Of course, Mother didn't understand how a child of hers could be both academically *and* musically inept, or how much Cecil hated being surpassed by not one but *two* younger sisters. His way of fighting back was to disclaim that blood tie for quite a few years, at the same time gaining a much-needed sense of self-worth by closely identifying with his two brothers. Since they were "the best" in everything, he thought, it meant he too had value and worth. It took us a long time to recognize the depths of his feelings of inferiority because he seemed so happy in bragging about our accomplishments.

When I was ten, Mother decided to rejoin the work force. We kids were all in school, and now that the Depression was over there were things she and Daddy wanted to do: buy clothing, get a telephone, replace our worn furniture, fix up the house, give us music lessons. Mother had a long list of "wants." Daddy had been the sole breadwinner for years, but she felt the time had come for her to help.

We believed she really lucked out on her first job, for she was hired as secretary-bookkeeper for a Mr. Crosier, the owner of the local ice company. She was thrilled to finally find work in an office; for years the only work open for colored women in Elkhart had been as domestics. Mother had graduated from Elkhart Business University, so she had all the skills necessary for the position. And it was only a ten-minute walk from the house on Lafayette Street to the office, which was on Harrison Street, just on the outer edges of the Italian community.

Mr. Crosier was a gentleman, a fine Christian, and totally unprejudiced. Mother's color mattered not at all to him; in fact, I think he felt this was a God-given opportunity to show his Christianity toward his fellow man. More important, and unfortunately, it *did* matter to Daddy, and he raged, stormed, and screamed. He didn't want *his* wife working in a one-girl office with a boss who

(counterclockwise from top left) Cecil, age twenty-one; Leah, age eighteen (high school yearbook, used by permission of Elkhart Community Schools); Stanley, age thirty-five.

was white! Mother seemed to have no choice but to quit that job—not just to keep the peace, but to hold the family together. I was shocked when, a very short time later, she started working for *Mrs. Crosier* in their home as a domestic!

Now, there's nothing in the world wrong with working as a domestic. It is hard, honest work, though its practitioners are usually grossly underpaid. Many colored women have supported entire families and even sent their children to college while working as housekeepers, laundresses, cooks, and cleaning persons. But here was an educated woman, repeatedly telling Leah and me that we should always aim for something higher, to get an education in the event anything ever happened to our husbands that might necessitate our having to support our families. By getting an education, we would be able to work at something other than scrubbing people's floors for a living!

She left out an important part of the equation: marry someone who recognizes your freedom to choose the work you do. It is choice, not chance, that often determines our destiny. I have often wondered if Mother and Daddy's marriage could or would have withstood the test of her being able to utilize her mental faculties in a more meaningful way. What would the result have been if she had stayed in that position at the ice company? Did Daddy feel it would make her—even with five children—a more independent spirit, less dependent on him?

I know the thought of "losing control" over Mother, even for a forty-hour work week and good pay, was abhorrent to him. The fact that Mr. Crosier was white made Daddy feel inferior. Even his great admiration for white people couldn't overcome his hidden feelings that any white man would take advantage of a colored woman, particularly if they were around each other every day. Too, he may not have fully trusted Mother.

Cecil (age four) and Shirley (age three)
in Grandma Morgan's front yard.

Pets

Daddy didn't want us to have pets because we might get so attached to them that if something happened to them we would be too upset. So, while we yearned for a puppy, a kitten, or a rabbit, *anything*, we certainly never thought it would happen to us.

We had been invited for dessert at the home of Mr. Weldy, our elementary school principal, after appearing on a program at their church. The Weldy boys had rabbits in their backyard, which absolutely fascinated all of us. We clustered around the rabbit hutches, and one of the Weldy boys even took a rabbit out and let Charles hold him.

Then, wonder of wonders, the Weldy sons, seeing how much we were enjoying the bunnies, persuaded Daddy to let them give us two rabbits, and even included a hutch in which to keep them! To Daddy, this was a white man presenting a gift, and he was not about to do what he considered "getting out of place" by refusing it, no matter how much he might want to. We didn't care what his reasons for accepting were; we simply wanted those rabbits.

Stanley and Cecil were especially happy about this, and it was quickly decided between them that the brown female would belong to Stanley and the snowy-white male would belong to Cecil. Overcoming a feeble attempt at refusal on Daddy's part, the Weldy boys pointed out to Daddy that since the hutch was divided, there wouldn't be a proliferation of bunny babies! I could see the wheels turning in Daddy's head: he'd have to provide food for those rabbits. To our amazed appreciation, though, we were also given several bags of rabbit food. The Weldys even loaded up the hutch into their pickup truck and hauled it home for us, so Daddy couldn't offer any more objections. Without further ado, "Brownie" and "Whitey" were installed in our backyard.

Mother gave us bowls for each rabbit's water, and we were allowed to give them, on occasion, lettuce and carrots to supplement their diet. Stanley and Cecil had the responsibility of cleaning up any and all rabbit droppings, and surprisingly, they performed this task daily with no grumbling.

Things were going well, and we enjoyed discovering the different personalities of the two rabbits. Whitey was very friendly and outgoing, and even though he would hop quickly out of the cage when it was opened, there was never a problem when it became time for him to be lifted up, given a quick hug, and put back in the cage. Brownie was not as trusting, and generally had to be coaxed out by putting a choice piece of lettuce in front of her. The two seemed to ignore the fact that they were side by side and of opposite sex, for they didn't make any overtures toward each other.

One Saturday afternoon while we were attending a youth meeting at church, a dog belonging to the large family living across the street went into our backyard, unfastened the hutch with his nose, and killed both rabbits when they hopped out. Brownie evidently was killed immediately, while Whitey was just barely alive when we returned home and went out to see how the rabbits were doing. Mother bandaged him and tried to repair the damage as we stood and watched with tears streaming down our faces.

Daddy was right, we kids *were* grief-stricken, for the next morning when we went running to the box in which Mother had placed Whitey, we found he too had died. Daddy admonished the boys sternly, "Remember, boys don't cry. Be a man, and don't ever show such a sign of weakness as crying." I can still see Cecil, eyes brimming with tears as he manfully tried to swallow his sobs.

But he didn't have to weep; Leah and I cried enough for all of us. *Our* crying was okay with Daddy because, after all, we were girls, and everybody knows girls, being the "weaker sex," cry more easily. Daddy got rid of the hutch, Mother retrieved her bowls, and it was as though we'd never known the pleasures of at last having pets of our own.

Just before Easter, when pet stores were still allowed to sell baby chicks, the boys bought three that had been tinted (with food coloring) in shades of purple, aqua, and blue. This purchase was Charles's idea, and I don't know why he thought Daddy would let us keep the chicks, but he had a plan: "If he says no, we can take them over to Grandma's; she'll let us keep them over there!"

Fascinated by the antics of the fluffy little chicks, we hovered over the box they were in and probably handled them too much, for two of them succumbed in very short order. The exception was the one belonging to Charles. He was named Peet-A-Wee after a pet chicken Mother had owned as a child, and he grew up to be a beautiful rooster, pure white when his feathers grew out, strong and cocky (pardon the pun!).

Once the chick was past babyhood, Charles lost interest in him, but that rooster and Leah *loved* each other. She would sit on the front porch, and Peet-A-Wee would hop up on her lap and stay there for hours as she stroked his feathers and "talked" to him, his head cocked to first one side and then the other, eyes bright and his red cockscomb alert, just as though he comprehended every word she spoke. I believe he did understand that Leah loved him; animals know and respond to affection, just as people do.

On summer mornings a little neighbor girl, Joan, often came to play with Leah; other times Leah would go to her house. This particular day we heard Joan out on the sidewalk calling Leah to come out and play—neither one ever knocked on the door—but then her voice became a frantic, panic-stricken cry for "LEAH! LEAH!" We all rushed outside just in time to see Joan streaking for home with Peet-A-Wee chasing after her and pecking at her legs. He must have scored a couple of hits, too, for we could see blood running down her leg. The big white rooster had become a watchdog!

A few days later, Mother gathered all of us together and told us we wouldn't be able to keep Peet-A-Wee at home anymore, for he might really hurt someone, or wander out in the road and be hurt himself. Mother said we were going to take him out to Uncle John's farm, where he could be with other chickens and farm animals. She also said he would be happier being the cock of the barnyard, ruling over the hens already in residence. But Leah cried her eyes out when we left him there; she was quite inconsolable.

A few weeks passed before we got a call from Uncle John. Seemingly, Peet-A-Wee would have nothing to do with the hens or other chickens, nor would he eat. Then, Uncle John said, he just went off into a corner of the barnyard and sat quietly by himself; nothing seemed to break through his lethargy. Finally, Uncle John told us, one morning when he had gone out to feed the chickens, he found Peet-A-Wee sitting all alone, head listing to one side, and he was gone: he had grieved himself to death. I believe Peet-A-Wee thought not only that he was a person, but that he was Leah's baby, and he could not bear being away from his mama.

That was our last pet, may he rest in peace! He had filled a special need for Leah: something she could love, show affection to, and that would love her unconditionally in return. While it was true Charles had bought him, Peet-A-Wee definitely was *her* chicken.

The Bicycle

That summer our parents bought a new bike for Leah and me to share, a shiny blue-and-white Goodyear with cushy tires that made for a smooth ride even over bumps, a wire basket in front to carry things, and a headlight for riding in dim light.

It was a typical summer Sunday afternoon in Indiana. Mother and Daddy were upstairs taking a nap; at least, that's what we thought they were doing because their bedroom door was closed and we didn't hear sounds of anyone talking. Leah and I went outside to take turns riding the new bike around the block. Everything went fine for a turn or two, but then Leah refused to let me have *my* turn. Now, Daddy had always cautioned us, "Don't any of you kids try to correct each other. If one of you does something wrong, tell me or your mother, and *we* will handle the situation."

So I went inside and called up the staircase, telling them Leah wasn't sharing the bicycle and was refusing to let me have my turn. Back outside I went, but each time I tried to get the bike from Leah she just laughed and rode off again. Three times I had to call upstairs to our parents. Suddenly, Mother came rushing down the stairs in her nightgown. She picked up a metal flyswatter lying on a nearby chair and started beating me up and down my back. Now, this was no ordinary flyswatter; it was made of heavy wire a bit thicker than a coat hanger, bent double all around, with one end holding a rubber mat to hit flies with. It was definitely not something with which to punish your child.

Oh God, how it hurt! I had never felt such excruciating pain. It was dreadful, and she seemed so totally unable to stop that I cried out for Daddy to come save me. The next thing I knew, he came flying down the stairs, yelling at Mother to stop. I had never before seen him so angry. "Where's Leah?" he demanded, with fire in his eyes and his lips quivering. "*She's* the one being disobedient, the one who should be getting punished, not Shirley!"

Mother, too, could tell he was positively livid with anger, and when he stormed by her, she playfully tapped *him* with the flyswatter in an attempt to defuse the situation and laughingly said, "Oh, Bill, you can't tell *me* who I can whip, I can even whip *you* with this if I want to!"

Daddy stopped abruptly, grabbed her arm, and told her, "Listen, Camille, don't play with me! It was Leah who was wrong, and *she* should be getting the punishment!" In the meantime, Leah had taken off and hidden somewhere, and she couldn't be found. (A good run is always better than a bad stand.)

Mother later said she had been afraid Daddy might seriously hurt Leah if he had been able to get his hands on her right then. I don't know what she called the pain she had just inflicted on me.

By the time Leah resurfaced, peace of a sort had been restored between Mother and Daddy, so she never got even a spanking, which I thought dreadfully unfair.

Hurt and upset, I went outside and sat on the back steps, sniffling and crying until the pain began to subside. I cried for the hurting, but even more for the deeper pain of what I felt was injustice. I had only done what they had told us all to do when one of us needed correcting. This, I had never expected from Mother, while a sense of fair play and justice had seemed always to have been built into Daddy (except, perhaps, where it concerned Stanley). This was why I had cried out to him. He alone, I felt, would see the injustice of it and could make Mother stop this unwarranted physical punishment.

If I had been in the wrong, I'm certain I would have felt I deserved a spanking, even if it hurt me physically. I had never before seen Mother in such a frenzied state as when she beat me—for it was indeed a beating, not a spanking.

The next day while I was taking my bath, Mother came in as usual to scrub my back. "What are all these black marks up and down your back?" she asked.

I glanced over my shoulder, then replied, "That's where you beat me yesterday with the flyswatter."

"Oh, go on, I didn't hit you *that* hard," she pooh-poohed me.

Now, added to the pain and unfairness of that beating, was the fact that she hadn't even realized the extent of the damage she had done, both to my body and to my young mind. What a wonderful thing it would have been if only she had said "I'm sorry," but she not only didn't, she never mentioned or discussed this episode again—not then, and not ever for the duration of my childhood years.

Many years passed before I reminded Mother of that beating. Oh yes, she remembered it, all right. She gave as her reason that she had been under a lot of stress at that time in her life. I, grown up by then, felt she had reacted that way because I had disturbed her and Daddy when they were indulging in sex: it would never have occurred to me back then, for children don't think of their parents doing things like that.

With tears in her eyes she begged my forgiveness, and I was genuinely able to forgive her because I realized we all do make mistakes at times, and that one had been hers. That beating, done today, would have qualified her for child abuse charges. It had also made me vow that if ever I had children, I would *never* beat or hit them in anger, which was a leap of the spirit ahead in time. Regardless of any mistakes I may have made in rearing my two daughters, beating them while I was mad wasn't one of them!

Mother had once told me that when she was a young girl she had been punished for something she had not done. Grandpa, possessed of a tremendous sweet tooth, could "smell" one of Grandma's pies and search it out, regardless of where or how well it might be hidden. This particular day Grandma had baked a pie to take to a church function and, carefully hiding it, told Mother not to let anyone touch it. Unbeknownst to Mother, Grandpa smelled the pie, located it, and ate half before returning it to its hiding place.

When Grandma came in and found the half-eaten pie, she immediately accused Mother because, she said, Mother was the only one who knew where it was. Grandpa just sat there, knowing full well he was the guilty party, while Grandma wore out a peach-tree switch on Mother despite her tearful protestations of innocence.

Mother never forgot that unjust punishment, which was another reason I couldn't understand her failure to realize how she had marked not only my body but my very soul. It is, of course, quite possible that in a twisted manner of thinking, Mother felt that none of her children should be above suffering as she once had, even though it had been unjustified. Even when a child is able to bury a memory behind and beneath other incidents, that injustice rankles beneath the surface for the rest of his or her life.

We tend to do to our children what was done to us, unless we have the love, the courage, the willpower to change our responses.

The Budding Writer

Somewhere around the age of ten or eleven I decided to try my hand at writing short stories. I had already written some poetry and wanted to do something different. But there was one short story I'll never forget; it was that first effort that caused me to experience other people's critiques. It also reinforced something I learned in later years, which was the advice to "write about what you know." If I had known of and heeded those words, I could have saved myself a lot of heartache.

I wrote my story on index cards and decided also to illustrate certain actions in it, even though I was not adept at drawing the human anatomy. I suppose I was beginning to be curious about sex, for this story was about the love life of two scantily clad trapeze artists and the embraces they shared as they flew through the air. What they performed on the high wire would not only have been miraculous, it would have been a physical impossibility! I thought, "Hmmm, there's poetic license. I'll try 'writer's license,' and then I can make my characters do whatever I want them to," a perfect example of my ignorance of the writer's craft. Certainly I knew next to nothing about my subject matter.

Knowing there was no place in the house to keep my cards away from my nosy brothers, I decided to keep them in my small green leather purse, which I would be taking to church with me on this particular Saturday. I felt my cards were safe, for I carried that purse with me always, and Leah's purse and mine were supposed to be off-limits to them.

On our way home from church we stopped for our usual short visit with our grandparents, since they lived a block from the church and we passed right by there. Leaving my purse unattended on Grandma's dining room table, I went into the kitchen for a glass of water. WRONG MOVE. Just as quickly as that, almost as though they had been watching me, the boys rummaged through my purse.

The next thing I knew, Charles and Cecil were standing beside me with looks of amused consternation on their faces, and the first words from Charles's mouth were, "Ooooh boy, are you in trouble. You are really gonna get it!"

My hand froze on the faucet, all desire for water completely gone. "Why?" I managed to croak out.

"Me and Cecil found some cards in your purse with dirty pictures on them, and when we showed them to Mother, she got *really* mad at you!"

I couldn't believe this invasion of my privacy, let alone their having the audacity to reveal their discoveries. My heart sank down to the soles of my feet as I entered the living room. All I could see was Mother's face with taut, thinned lips and an extremely angry expression. All her freckles were standing out like golden dots as she commanded: "We're all going home *right now.*" We went. Usually we conversed with each other on the walk home, but this day not a word was spoken. The return trip seemed to have been completed in double-time, for it ended much too quickly.

With little appetite and a great deal of apprehension, I barely pecked at our Sabbath meal, expecting that Mother would report me to Daddy while we were all at the dinner table, since that seemed to be the favored place for revealing our misdeeds and meting out our punishments. Spankings and beatings while eating dinner were quite common occurrences, although I had never before been the recipient. But she said nothing. I thought, "Maybe since it is the Sabbath, she won't tell on me until after sundown."

Daddy ate dinner, took his usual nap, and returned to work, apparently noticing nothing awry. After he left, Mother sent Leah and the boys upstairs and called me to sit down in the living room, speaking very formally. I knew the thunder and lightning were going to roll. I could see Charles and Cecil hovering at the head of the staircase, peeking through the banisters in an attempt to hear whatever was going to be said or done.

"So, missy, that's what you would do if you had the chance!" were her first accusing words, which was all it took for me to dissolve in a flood of tears. "What do you think your daddy is going to say about all of this when I tell him?"

At those words I begged, I implored her, "Mother, *please* don't tell Daddy about this!"

"Oh, yes, I can't keep something like this from him, I *must* tell him," Mother responded. "He's going to be so disappointed in you, that you would do such a thing! And to think you had the nerve to bring that smut, that filth, right into the house of the Lord. It's a wonder God didn't strike you dead!"

However, just at that moment I wasn't overly worried about God; I was more concerned about what Daddy would think and say. Fearfully I cast around in my mind to find something, anything that would ensure her silence. She was, however, implacable in her determination. Frantic, I ran upstairs to my room, the boys scattering back to their own bedroom. I tossed a few things into a suitcase and hurried back down to the front door, trying desperately to open it but hampered by the suitcase in my hand.

Mother looked up from the papers she was reading and asked, "And just where do you think you're going?"

"I'm gonna run away from home!" I shouted wildly, tears still streaming down my face as I finally succeeded in getting the door open.

Mother glanced at the suitcase and then at me. In a calm, matter-of-fact voice she said, "Well, missy, everything in that suitcase belongs to me because I bought and paid for them, so unless I permit it, you can't take them out of this house." Almost as an afterthought she queried further, "Just where do you think you're running off to?"

I threw down the suitcase. "I'm going over to live with Grandma and Grandpa!" I exclaimed. (Oh, what a haven of refuge our grandparents were!) I knew they would want me, regardless of what I might have done.

Continuing her perusal of the papers in her hand and not even getting up from her chair, she then told me: "Well, missy, you know the dress you have on, the underwear, your shoes, your socks, all belong to me too!" Of course she knew I wouldn't dare leave the house stark naked, so her words once more sent me into tearful paroxysms as I ran back to my room to await Daddy's arrival home that evening. I knew she would call me downstairs while she reported my wrongdoing.

I truly didn't want Daddy to change his high opinion of me, his pride in my accomplishments, or his love for his obedient little daughter. Musing silently, I asked myself, "Has what I've done been such a bad thing? After all, I was only trying to write a story!" It was a restless and uneasy night's sleep for me as I wondered when the call from Mother would come.

But it never did. The next day, Sunday, as we were doing the laundry, all Mother said was that she hadn't told Daddy because she, too, didn't want to spoil his opinion of me as a "nearly perfect" child. In Mother's eyes, my transgression was so sinful she couldn't bring herself to speak to Daddy about it. For once, I believed that "silence is golden," and it had definitely worked out in my favor!

I'm sure it was the pictures that attracted the most attention from my brothers, and I never again tried to be an illustrator. You can definitely believe that from that day forward my little green purse carried only innocuous items like tissue, a pencil, a compact, and a pack of gum. Nothing I wrote afterward needed to be hidden, although I failed to understand why the boys hadn't been reprimanded for their trespassing. Perhaps my transgression outdid theirs.

Chicago and Cousin Ora

A couple hours' ride on the westbound New York Central Railroad brought you to Chicago. To the Gordon kids, the most important thing about that city was not that it was big, but that it was where our Cousin Ora lived. The daughter of Grandmother's half-brother Uncle Horace (H. C. Ingram), she was one of the constants of our lives. How we all loved her, from our grandparents down to our sister Leah, for *she* loved us all, unconditionally! While Uncle Horace only cared for the family members who were dark-complexioned, Ora, although dark like her father, was truly color-blind.

Uncle Horace didn't like Grandfather, Aunt Bea, or Mother because they were too light. He exhibited extreme favoritism toward Mother's brother and sister, Uncle Al and Aunt Lula, because of their darker skin. With Leah, Cecil, and Stanley, he was quite talkative, but to Mother, Charles, and me, he had very little to say.

Whenever Aunt Lula came to visit from California, she would change from the Santa Fe Super Chief train to the New York Central, which left from the LaSalle Street station, in Chicago. Ora always met her at the Dearborn Street station, and they would spend several days together, visiting, laughing, and talking. Sometimes Ora would simply get on the train for Elkhart with Aunt Lula, full of plans for a great vacation and some time together. They loved going fishing together, yet I don't recall their ever catching anything.

It was the same for all of us, simply knowing Ora was always there for us. In fact, I used to vow that when I grew up I was going to get a job in Chicago and share an apartment with Ora, for I loved being around her just that much. She always made me feel this childish dream could very well come true: "Shirley-girl, we'll plan on it, if you still feel that way when you finish college." As far as I was concerned, it was etched in stone.

It was Ora who told us many stories about things we had done as really little kids. We particularly liked the story she told about

Charles and Stanley when they were three and two years old, respectively. Charles, fairer-complexioned, had hair that wasn't quite straight, while Stanley, brown-skinned, had beautiful curly black hair. One day while Ora, Mother, and Grandmother were visiting in the kitchen, they realized they hadn't heard any sounds from the boys for a while. Ora jumped up and went looking for them. She opened the walk-in closet in the downstairs bedroom (Grandpa's infamous closet), only to discover Charles had taken scissors and was busily at work cutting Stanley's curls! He had evidently become jealous of hearing people exclaim over how pretty Stanley's hair was. Mother cried, but it was too late by then, so Stanley had to get his first "real" haircut.

Ora was always amused at Charles's inventiveness, even at such a tender age, in being able to get what he wanted. Charles never liked to share the spotlight with his siblings, either then or in later years. If he couldn't have the prettiest hair, by golly, he'd surely see to it that Stanley's was no longer his crowning glory. So far as he was concerned, *he* was Mother's only child, and he would not let attention be diverted from him, for he was the star.

Ora had two brothers and numerous cousins, all of whom lived in Elkhart. Of them all, Ora was the one with the outgoing personality, the vivaciousness, the kindness of heart that made everyone love her. I often wondered how she could be Uncle Horace's daughter, yet be so loving to every one of us. I've also wondered how, since the blood connection was so distant, my sister, Leah, looked as though *she* could have been Ora's daughter; both tall and slender, their body size and leg shapes were identical. Whereas Leah later grew resentful because of her color, it never seemed to occur to Ora that she and Leah were of a darker complexion. In fact, none of us thought about it; to us she was always simply our beloved Cousin Ora, even to Charles, who was quick—especially in his teen years—to add a slight nuance of disdain toward darker people.

Ora was the first person we knew of from Elkhart who had attended the renowned Tuskegee Institute in Alabama after high school graduation. She then moved to Chicago to seek employment, because Elkhart was still a "no-man's land" for colored women who wanted to break out of the "domestics" mold. I don't know what kind of job she had, although in later years she became a licensed practical nurse. I believe the character of Cora in *No Place to Be Somebody* was patterned after her. She always worked, and she had a nice apartment, a varied wardrobe, and several boyfriends, with enough money to do whatever she pleased.

When I was in my mid-teens, Ora fell in love with a fellow named Roberson. Plans were made for a June wedding to be held at Canaan Baptist Church, where she had been a member and her father had long been a deacon. I was proud to be asked to play the piano for the wedding, while Stanley was asked to be one of the groom's attendants. The groom's sister, who lived and worked in Johannesburg, South Africa, came all the way to Elkhart to be Ora's maid of honor.

The bride was lovely, the groom handsome, and everything went off smoothly, but something was nagging at me and I *had* to ask Ora about it: would her getting married mean I couldn't live with her when I finished college? Ora thought that was the funniest thing she'd ever heard, and she laughingly reassured me that there would always be room for me, regardless of where she lived. None of us knew at that point that by the time I finished college, Ora would be a divorcee; she never seemed to have much success with her boyfriends, but it certainly never dampened her spirits or kept her from trying to find " Mr. Wonderful."

Ora kept an immaculate apartment and was as good a cook as Grandmother or Mother. I loved her quick wit, her great sense of humor, and the love she exhibited when she greeted all of us kids, from Charles down to Leah, with a big smile and warm hugs all around. Charles bloomed around Ora, for she paid a lot of attention to him, saying all the things that stroked his young ego.

Uncle Horace was a retired railroad man, and he was able to provide Ora with a pass so she could come home to Elkhart whenever she wanted to, which was never often enough for us. As soon as Charles saw Ora, he'd ask, "What do you want me to sing for you?" She was never too busy or distracted to sit and listen to him, and she took the same interest in all of our doings. It was not uncommon to see her in the big swing on Grandma's front porch, all of us crammed in around her, busily laughing and talking at once. It was as though each of us was her child.

It was because of Ora that we started going to Chicago on weekends. We went to the large church there on Saturday, but Sunday was our "fun day." Upon returning home we talked so much about the fun we'd had that Daddy began to get a bit jealous. You can imagine the babble of five kids all wanting to tell about the things they had seen, what they had learned, where they had gone. Daddy began telling Mother that as our parents, *they* should be the ones to take this interest in us.

So, at least two or three times in the summer, Daddy would wake us early on Sunday with the words, "Get up, we're taking the train to Chicago." Always, Charles's first question was "Are we going to see Ora?" It wasn't until we arrived that we discovered where we were going: perhaps the Field Museum of Natural History, maybe the Shedd Aquarium, or even the Museum of Science and Industry. One of our favorite places was the Brookfield Zoo. It was especially nice when we went to a place called Riverside Amusement Park, where they had all kinds of rides, sideshows, game booths, roller coasters, and other entertainment. We could always count on Ora going on a ride with one of us if we were scared to go alone.

Ora would be waiting for us at the Englewood Station near Sixty-third and State streets, since it was closest to where she lived. She would give us directions on how to reach our destination, assuming she didn't just come along with us. It always heightened our enjoyment when she did, for she was truly a fun person to be around. She had a special and unconditional love for us that was missing from our everyday lives, and we responded to it totally.

In the center of the main entrance hall at the Field Museum, there were two bull elephants preserved in a fighting stance. My brothers always ran to look at them first, as though they could be missed. Once we saw these elephants, we knew we were really there. The exhibits were so lifelike you easily imagined being right there, almost as though you were on safari.

We could sometimes fit in a trip to the Shedd Aquarium on the same day as the Field Museum, for it was just across the way. The Adler Planetarium, also close by, gave lectures on the heavens and the stars, but I didn't enjoy it as much in later years because of my hearing loss; once the house lights dimmed I couldn't follow what was being said.

Brookfield Zoo, located a bit outside the city limits, meant an exciting ride on the electric train, and I think it was our favorite trip. Mother packed a big picnic basket of fried chicken (our once-a-year treat), kidney bean salad, sandwiches, some fresh fruit, and a pie for dessert. We never even thought about how early she must have risen to prepare this ahead of time. As soon as we arrived, Daddy put the basket in a storage locker so he wouldn't have to lug it all around, for the zoo covered quite a number of acres. It was one of the first zoos in the country to build quarters for the animals that were as close to their native habitats as possible.

We looked forward to seeing Monkey Island and wanted this to be our first stop, before we saw any of the other animals. We would rush over there excited, eyes alight, ready to see what the monkeys were up to. The exhibit was truly an island, with a mountain in the center that was completely surrounded by a moat and had trees and vines for the monkeys to swing from. Monkeys everywhere! Daddy didn't care for the monkeys because they had no hair on their backsides, which he found disgusting and most evident when they stood up or swung through the air.

Charles had a method to get the monkeys' attention. He had some kind of chatter, vocalized sounds which he'd "speak" to them; it was amazing how many of them would line up, seemingly listen, then chatter back to him. We teased him unmercifully—"Yeah, you're talking to your relatives"—but he didn't care: he shrugged and said they were more fun than the "monkeys" he had to live with at home.

Usually long before we kids were ready, Daddy would be champing at the bit to move on to other animals, so we left most reluctantly. Nothing else absorbed us as did the monkeys, but we looked at them anyway: lions, tigers, elephants, antelope, rhinos, and hippopotamuses, and we really did learn how they lived in their native habitats. The boys also looked forward to going inside the snake and reptile house, but Leah and I had no interest in those creatures, and were only too glad they were securely enclosed in glass cages. Quite naturally, being boys, this was our brothers' favorite stop, second only to seeing the monkeys.

Around noon we returned to the storage locker to pick up the food, which Mother would spread out on a nearby picnic table. On these occasions Daddy would buy each of us a bottle of soda, never allowed any other time, for he said the carbonated beverage would aid our digestion. We didn't care why, we just enjoyed.

Upon our return to Elkhart, pleasantly tired from all the excitement, fresh air, and walking around, we knew that before the day was over Daddy would make his favorite pronouncement: "You kids go places very few white children get to go, and no niggers at all!" We were always surprised to see other colored families with children in tow, obviously having just as good a time as we were; we thought *we* would be the only colored people there. After all, hadn't Daddy said "*No* niggers at all?" The sneaking suspicion began to enter our childish minds that maybe Daddy wasn't always right, but it was something we never dared voice, not even amongst ourselves. Silence on that possibility was more than golden; it was platinum.

Those trips to Chicago, always a joy for us, lived in our hearts ever after, inextricably woven into memories of Ora and our good times there. We were aware in our hearts that if it hadn't been for Cousin

Ora, those trips would probably never have occurred. Thanks to her, we had some days and times when we were carefree children, times we were loved just for being us, and times when an adult seemed to enter wholeheartedly into sharing our world, our happiness. To us, Ora and Chicago were inseparable.

The Nightmare

One night we were all sleeping soundly, when suddenly Charles awakened us screaming. He had not been feeling well that day, so Mother had made up a bed downstairs on the living room sofa for him. His shrieks reverberated through the house, sending chills up and down our spines as we tumbled out of bed and raced downstairs. Something terrible must surely be the matter. We heard him cry out, "Oh, no, no, no, no, my golden egg is broken, and I'm dying!"

As fast as we were, Mother beat us all down there. Charles was crying, and Mother was holding him in her arms as she pleaded, "Charles, Charles, you're a sinner! Please ask God to forgive you for your sins before you die!"

Gulping for air, Charles managed to gasp, "God, please forgive me!"

Mother ran to put on her robe and raced to the neighbors to make two phone calls, since we didn't have a phone: one to the doctor, the other to Grandmother to tell her Charles was dying. The four of us stood around on various levels of the staircase, crying our eyes out, while Daddy sat beside Charles and held his hand until Mother returned.

Although it was two o'clock in the morning, our good Dr. Todd arrived very quickly and examined Charles, who was by now wide awake. After putting his thermometer and stethoscope away, Dr.

Todd turned to Mother and said, "Well, he doesn't have a fever, and his chest sounds are normal. I think he's just had a bad dream, a nightmare. Keep an eye on him for a day or two, make him rest, drink lots of liquids, and he should be fine. But call me anytime if you feel you need me."

Dr. Todd was one of the very few white doctors in town who would accept colored patients. He treated them just as he did his other patients, even letting them come to his office during regular office hours and enter through the front door. We had a tremendous amount of respect for him and his medical expertise.

As the doctor turned to leave, poor Grandmother arrived—out of breath, teary-eyed, and scared stiff. Not having a car, she had run the entire distance to our house, which was several miles of dirt road with no streetlights. She flew over to Charles and hugged and kissed him. When she understood that he was going to be all right, she collapsed into the nearest chair, pulled her apron over her face, and began to cry unrestrainedly, while Daddy awkwardly patted her on the shoulder until she regained control. He was unaccustomed to displaying any emotion; men didn't, he always maintained, but he surely evinced a bit of tenderness that night.

Charles shamefacedly told us that he had dreamed he had a goose that laid a golden egg, but someone had picked it up and broken it all into pieces. He was soon up and about, but we were all very subdued for several days, thinking how awful it would have been if he had died, but overjoyed that he hadn't.

Shortly after that time, I often wondered just how much of a sinner a twelve-year-old boy could be that would warrant Mother making such extravagant statements to him on what she thought might be his deathbed. None of us had done any of the things we had been admonished by Mother for years not to do: we hadn't "broken the Sabbath"; we went regularly to church and studied our Sabbath school lessons diligently; we followed the biblical injunction to "honor thy father and thy mother." We didn't attend the theater, or dance, or listen to "worldly" music, or dress immodestly. We didn't swear, and we treated our elders with respect.

Wracking my young brain for reasons, the only thing I could come up with was taking those chunks of ice off the iceman's truck when he wasn't looking. It had to be that we were thieves; eventually God would strike us dead or, even worse, consign us to hell. We felt Charles's "narrow escape" from death was meant to serve as a warning to the rest of us, and so we determined we had to try living closer to God so that maybe, just maybe, we might escape punishment. What a pious bunch of mournful-faced little kids we were for quite a while after that.

Sisters

Multitalented Mother decided to redo the kitchen, and like most of the things she did, it was very successful. Daddy put new rubber asphalt tile on the floor, then "let" Mother paint the kitchen a soft white, with interiors of red inside the cupboards and drawers. It was early summer, school was out, and Mother had done this remarkable job in just a few days. How different it all looked!

On this particular day it was my turn to dry dishes after Leah washed them. Opening a drawer to place clean cooking utensils away, I noticed some letters crudely scratched in the still-soft enamel on an upper edge of one of the drawers: "IHTND." Puzzled, I didn't know just what it meant or who would have done such a thing. I couldn't imagine Mother defacing something on which she had labored so mightily. I mulled this over in my mind, and then suddenly it hit me: I knew exactly what the letters stood for.

That evening after supper, it was my turn to wash and Leah's to dry. Our parents were relaxing in the other room, their dishwasher operating busily out in the kitchen: nothing automatic about it, *we* were the dishwashers. I turned to Leah and asked, "Why did you scratch those letters into the paint on that drawer?" and pointed to the incriminating evidence. Leah looked, shrugged her shoulders, and turned away, feigning ignorance, but I was determined not to let her get away with this.

"I know what it means, too," I asserted. "It stands for 'I Hate That Nigger Dad!'"

Leah's eyes widened, her mouth fell open, and she jumped as though someone had stuck her with a pin. In a loud whisper she exclaimed, "How did you figure that out?"

"I'm right, too, aren't I?" I persisted, and she had grace enough to hang her head as she nodded limply. "Don't tell on me, please!" she pitifully begged.

I thought for a moment. "Well, you know how he sees *everything,* so if he sees it, you'll have to confess, because I don't want him or Mother to think I did this!" I shut the drawer emphatically, sure I had made my point.

The next day I opened that drawer to get a spatula. I could hardly believe my eyes: each letter had been carefully scraped away, down to the bare wood, and was now illegible. A day or so later Mother saw the raw space and retouched it; I suppose she thought she had missed a spot. Good as new! Daddy never saw it, and I was surely not going to tell him what his own daughter thought of him.

This was just the beginning of Leah's outward displays of inner dislike, distaste, and hatred toward both of her parents, but especially toward Daddy. She hated the punishments he meted out and hated Mother for not saving her from—or at least intervening in—some of it. She, like the rest of us, felt a mother was supposed to love, care for, and protect her children, and when this did not happen we all felt emotionally abandoned and deprived. It was as though Mother wanted to placate Daddy at all costs, despite the effect it was having on our young minds and bodies. Food, shelter, and clothing can never replace the need for at least one nurturing parent. But

Sisters: Shirley at age nine (*left*) and Leah at five.
Courtesy of Alexander Tschumakow.

Leah's disobedience frequently brought down a lot of punishment on her own head.

Leah and I were supposed to share the housework, but she seldom did her part without frequent prodding and reminders from me. One afternoon in particular, I was trying to get everything done before our parents got home. Instead of helping, she was lying on the floor in the living room, laughing aloud over the comics, totally ignoring my demands for help every time I had to step over her. I must have reminded her once too often, because suddenly she sprang up from the floor and lit into me. She pulled my hair, yanking out a long strand that was as big around as my little finger. She scratched and bit. She won. I finished the cleaning in silence, alone.

Now, Leah had a history of beating up on me because I wouldn't fight back; after all, I was three years older and she was the "baby." If I did hit her, I would stand there waiting for her to hit me back; then I would dissolve into tears and the fight was over. We had always been admonished to let Mother or Daddy handle any corrections or punishments when needed, and this time was no exception. I carefully saved the strand of hair to show Mother the minute she came in.

Was I ever in for a surprise! After I told her what happened, she walked right by me, through the dining room and kitchen, and out of the back door into the yard. When she returned, she had a switch in her hand from which she was stripping the leaves. She then called us to come into the dining room, where she waited for us.

We stood there, never before having seen this and wondering what was going to happen next. Well, *we* were! "Now, girls, you want to fight, I'm going to see that you do it. Shirley, I'm sick and tired of coming home to hear you crying that Leah has beaten you up; Leah, I'm fed up with you and your bullying attitude when you know Shirley won't fight back. You want to fight? Okay, you two are going to fight while I watch, and if you don't, I'm going to use this switch on *both* of you."

Our mouths were hanging open in shock; we were being told to *fight?* But we believed her. In any event, I'd rather have gotten beaten up by Leah than switched by Mother, so I lit in, taking a page from Leah's fight book. I hit, I bit, I kicked and scratched, and I didn't give her a chance to land a blow. For the first time ever I was on the offensive. This time it was Leah who dissolved in tears, turning pitifully to Mother and asking, "Did you see what she did?"

Mother simply stood there watching as I snatched and pulled Leah's hair. Again Leah tearfully asked, "Did you see what she did? She *hit* me! She pulled my hair!"

Cool as a cucumber, Mother replied: "Yes, and she saved her own skin by doing so, while *you've* gotten your own well-deserved punishment. Now, let this be a lesson to you both: NO FIGHTING!"

Boy, the old adrenaline was pumping! I, who hated any type of physical confrontation or violence, had actually won a fight. What a feeling! Over the past several years Leah had grown heavier and a couple of inches taller than me, so she was now physically bigger, but I had literally brought her to her knees. It was a tremendous boost to my ego. From that day on, Leah never wanted to physically engage me again. I hadn't just won the battle; I'd won the war.

Black Belt

A worn black leather belt hung on the knob behind the dining room door. It had once been used to hold up Daddy's pants, but now, with the buckle broken and removed, it was used solely as an instrument of punishment. Mother used it to give us beatings, and it was the only thing Daddy ever used to give my brothers a lashing; he never used his hand, a hairbrush, or a switch, just that black belt. When he finished, it was always returned to that doorknob to hang in solitary confinement until one of them needed it again. With one end of the belt wrapped around a hand, either parent could and did deal some smashing blows that left welts and, on occasion, bleeding.

Sometimes when we felt someone was on the verge of getting a beating, one of us would sneak and hide it; Daddy invariably used it while we were all at the dinner table and would send one of us to "go get that belt." This was usually Cecil or me, since we sat closest to the door. How we hated having to deliver that weapon of destruction to him! He never caught on to our occasional hiding of the belt, so on several occasions a beating didn't materialize because we conveniently couldn't locate it, knowing he would not use anything else.

Stanley was about nine years old when Daddy began seriously picking on him. Grandma once told me that of all the boys, Stanley was the spitting image of his biological father, so perhaps Daddy saw him as a reminder of Mother's ex-husband, Charles Fleming. Daddy wasn't educated enough to know how to deal with his jealousy, although I admit I have found education no guarantee against having that old green-eyed serpent rear its ugly head! It might also have been as simple as doing it because he could, knowing Mother would say nothing against it, at least not in front of us; if this was something they argued about behind closed doors, we never heard about it, and it certainly continued to happen.

The punishments affected the rest of us too, not only Stanley. You don't have to be the one receiving the blows, or bearing the marks and scars, to become traumatized by witnessing severe and often bloody discipline inflicted on those whom you love.

Mealtimes were the worst. Our main meal was dinner, which we ate at noon because Daddy felt it was more healthful. In a small town like Elkhart, it wasn't too far for us all to come home, eat, and walk back to school. Even when we were in high school, Daddy insisted on us doing that to ensure we ate what was good for us.

There wasn't one of us who didn't *hate* dinnertime—in spite of the good food Mother prepared—because of the tension, anger, and hatred that seemed to erupt. We all sat there, tense and nervous, wondering when the ax would fall and one of us, usually Stanley or Leah, would be the recipient of Daddy's wrath. It was at dinnertime that Daddy would force Stanley to eat the spinach that was put on his plate and that Stanley absolutely hated, so much so that it made him gag. He knew there was no way to avoid eating it, for we were all expected to eat everything that was set in front of us whether we liked it or not.

Often Daddy grabbed Stanley up and away from the table so he could have plenty of room to beat him with that black belt while continuing to force him to eat. I did have to smile on one occasion: Daddy was in such a hurry to beat Stanley he couldn't wait for Cecil or me to bring the belt, and he jerked his own belt off. When Daddy's pants started to fall, he became so busy pulling them back up that he lost some of his anger, and so that particular beating was averted.

Sometimes it would be Leah who brought down Daddy's wrath during the meal, and he would snatch her from her high chair, her little legs caught under the table, and give her a tremendous shaking before slamming her back down in her seat. I'm sure the rest of us looked like scared little rabbits as we sat around the table, wondering if someone else would be next. And Mother said not a word. In fact, she didn't even seem to see what was happening.

Things got so bad that I learned to read Daddy's face when we sat down at the table, trying to determine what kind of mood he was in. If we saw his lip quiver or curl, we *all* watched out. I began bringing to the table a little paper we got in elementary school called *My Weekly Reader,* folded unobtrusively and tucked behind me, open to a section in the back that contained jokes. If Daddy seemed irascible, I'd produce the paper and read a joke, for I had discovered if I could just get him to laugh, his bad mood would be dispelled and we could eat the remainder of the meal in relative peace and quiet.

These were, of course, simple and childish jokes, but I didn't care so long as they worked. And subtlety would never have done it. I absolutely hated it when I had to read all the jokes at one meal, for I'd then have to wait until the following week for a new edition: suppose in the interim there was another bad day? I saw Mother giving me a strange look one day after I had read a joke or two, and from her expression I could tell she knew what I was doing. Yet she seemed unable to actively help avert this turmoil, and never once did she say a word of remonstrance to Daddy.

Years later I discovered Charles, like me, actually got stomach pains when we were told dinner was ready. Stanley and Cecil said the same thing, while Leah swore it was a contributing factor in her development of ulcers at an early age.

Things became so bad between Daddy and Stanley that he began wetting the bed at night, something he hadn't done since he was a baby. Nothing seemed to help or to stop it. I lost count of the number of mornings we were all awakened by the sound of Daddy yelling, then Stanley's cries and the sounds of a belt hitting flesh. Daddy made it a special point to check Stanley's bed before anyone else was even awake.

After one such occurrence, Daddy put Stanley's cot down in the cold, dark basement, in a room without a light fixture, and made him sleep there with only a few newspapers spread around to serve as a cushion, covered with just a thin blanket and a very skimpy pillow. He said Stanley didn't deserve to sleep in a warm bedroom with the other boys, and perhaps this would teach him not to wet the bed. We all stood around and watched, with tears streaming down our faces, as Daddy made up this cot—but we knew better than to say anything.

Stanley was banished to that basement for over a week. Mother, too, stood by and watched, but she didn't shed one tear. Neither did she say one single word of remonstrance. This was not discipline: this was child abuse.

Yet we were expected to finish our meal or resume our activities after these interruptions just as though nothing had happened.

To Daddy, this was nothing out of the ordinary. To us, it was quite traumatic, and it was inscribed indelibly upon our young psyches. And it didn't seem to be discipline that had been administered; this was simply an adult striking out in a blind rage, intent on obtaining satisfaction by physically hurting someone unable to defend himself. The beatings lasted until his anger was spent, which was longer than it took Stanley to say, "I'm sorry" or "I'll try not to do that again."

One Sunday morning Daddy sent the boys upstairs to clean their bedroom. He was a firm believer in the boys taking an active part in doing household chores and not leaving it all up to Mother, and on this day he had decreed the window must be washed, the blankets aired, and the furniture thoroughly dusted and polished. This seemed like overkill to me because other than the bunkbeds and Stanley's cot, the room contained only one piece of furniture, a small dresser that had a few drawers for underwear and socks. It was such a wee room for three growing boys! Their closet measured only about four square feet, with no rod to hang clothing from, only a few nails driven into the wall.

Daddy even wanted the painted wooden floors to be mopped, which also seemed unnecessary to me since even after this was done, you couldn't tell any difference in the before and after. Since Daddy was the maintenance man for the YWCA, he thought he was the only one who knew exactly how these things should be done.

We'd finished Sunday breakfast when the boys got their marching orders, and they trooped upstairs with brooms, mops, and clean rags. Daddy had instructed them in precisely what he expected them to accomplish, so after a few minutes he went up to check on their progress. He carried a bucket of hot soapy water for mopping the floor, and from downstairs I could hear him set the bucket down with a thump.

The next thing I heard was someone screaming, the sounds of a scuffle, and exclamations of, "I *told* you how to do that; now you *do* it!" Not having the black belt handy, Daddy had grabbed Stanley and begun throwing him around the room. In the tussle Daddy overturned the bucket, and water flew everywhere. Then it became a mad scramble to get that water up off the floor, but it was too late; it had already seeped through the floorboards, and brown stains rapidly spread across the ceiling of the dining room directly below, which had been freshly wallpapered only a week before.

Oh, Daddy was furious! But for once he could only blame himself. What happened to that ceiling was his own fault, and out of sight and sound, I laughed my head off as I murmured to myself, "Serves you right, you big bully!" For of course he had to pay the wallpaperer to redo that ceiling, and I knew spending additional money was severe punishment for our thrifty daddy.

He still didn't understand the lesson involved in his treatment of Stanley: you can't hurt someone else without also hurting yourself. If he had simply applied the Bible's Golden Rule—to treat others as you would want to be treated—we would have led much more peaceful lives. But Daddy evidently believed that if he spared the rod he would spoil the child.

Paper Dolls

It took quite a large box—the one that Mother's new winter coat had come in—to hold all my paper dolls. I had been collecting them for years. There were movie-star dolls: Jane Withers, Deanna Durbin, Gene Tierney, Shirley Temple, Rita Hayworth; the Dionne quintuplets; Princesses Elizabeth and Margaret Rose; families composed entirely of baby dolls; airline stewardesses; even an adorable colored twin set, a boy named Patches and a girl named Petunia. Whenever Aunt Bea came from Chicago where she worked, she always brought me new additions for my collection. I haunted Kresge's, Woolworth's, and McClellan's dime stores for the newest arrivals. Some were given to me by the daughters of my parents' friends, and one in particular that was life-size had been given to me by a girl who lived in a little town called Lake Wawasee, whom we had met through our friendship with Principal Weldy, his wife, and Church of the Brethren members. I had to make the clothes for that doll myself, since the local stores didn't carry this larger doll, which stood as tall as I was at the time. That doll was always special because Charles used to pretend he was dancing with her—but not in front of Mother!

I spent hours carefully cutting out all their clothes, changing their outfits, and acting out my own little playlets. Sometimes Leah would play with the dolls and me, but she soon lost interest and would start handling them too roughly, causing them to bend, and then they would no longer stand up straight. I repeatedly warned her to be careful, but then she'd be bored and wander outside to see what the boys were doing, which was fine with me. Then I could make the dolls do and say whatever I wanted without having to explain the script, or worry about possible damage to my beloved dolls. Every one of them had a name.

Kept under my bed, the doll box was easily accessible for me to pull out and play with in my favorite spot on the landing at the head of the stairs. I tried to keep everything in that box, for Mother had told me that while she didn't care how much I played with them, I had to make sure everything was picked up and put away when I finished.

One day I missed a few small scraps, and when Mother came upstairs those bits and pieces were the first things she saw. Hastily I reached for them, but she grabbed them first, and then reached under the bed to yank out the box. Oh, if *only* she had merely pointed out that I had overlooked a few snippets! Instead, Mother crammed the top tightly onto the box and marched out of the room, down the stairs all the way to the basement, where, before my horrified eyes, she shoved the box and its entire contents into the furnace.

She then struck a match, and my beautiful, much-loved paper dolls became charred memories.

Turning to me, Mother said, "That's also what happens to little girls who don't mind what their mothers tell them. They burn up in the Lake of Fire, in hell. The Bible says so!"

I wasn't just crushed; I was devastated. Running upstairs to my room, I lay down and cried my small heart out. I couldn't have felt worse if the dolls had been human beings, for to me each one had her own personality, her own looks, her own persona.

I was only ten, but I was able to question how religion entered into what had just transpired. How could someone who was supposed to be a loving mother manifest that extreme kind of cruelty to a child's heart and mind? It was not just the power—because of course she was physically stronger than me—but her intense desire and terrible intent to hurt, with its successful conclusion that destroyed an innocent yet important part of my world. If this was love, the lesson made me want no part of it; therefore, I would close my ears to any and all declarations that it had been love for me that brought this about. Her insistence on complete control and exercise of power was what had fueled the flames of her actions, with a desire to hurt me as well.

Shortly afterward, while I was still sobbing on the bed, Charles came upstairs and gently patted me on the shoulder, saying over and over again, "It's all right, Shirley; it's all right." My heart was comforted to know that he, at least, understood my feelings and the hurt. It was the first time any of us had expressed concern and sympathy at an injustice from Mother, and while we could say nothing to her face, Charles always occupied a special place in my heart ever after. He knew the risk he was taking if Mother should hear him trying to comfort me.

From that day forward, I never again collected or played with paper dolls. One more door of escape from the harshness of our home life had been slammed shut in my face. And when Aunt Bea brought me new books of paper dolls, I thanked her for them but later went downstairs and burned them. You can believe neither Mother nor I ever told her what had transpired: me, because I was too hurt, and Mother, because it was unimportant to her. I believe, too, that Aunt Bea would have gotten very angry with Mother about it.

Years later, while sifting through some old photos, I came across one of Mother standing on our front porch, wearing a gray coat with a large fur collar. My first reaction was: "Oh, that's the coat that came in the box I kept my paper dolls in before Mother burned them in the furnace!" I turned it face-down, unable to look at it any longer, for the hurt had remained inside me for all those years.

Never once did she ever acknowledge any remorse for what she had done. It was as though she thought whatever she did was right, simply because she was the mother and we were her children, never supposed to question her actions. To Mother, it was only *her* opinions that mattered. But she totally lacked the understanding that wrongs are terribly impressed on young minds, indelibly and forever.

Several years after Charles had won the Pulitzer, Mother became incensed at his choice of career. It was not sufficient to simply stop having contact with him; she had to take her anger many steps further. How best to let him know that she highly disapproved of his lifestyle, that she considered it a total repudiation of all the mores and values taught by her and Daddy? For many years she had collected and saved all the news clippings, ribbons, medals, trophies, certificates, and photographs of his lifetime of activities: there were four shoe boxes full of memorabilia. Gathering up these things, she took them to the basement, jammed them into the furnace, and set fire to them. Needless to say, many of these items were irreplaceable.

In this same manner she had destroyed my paper dolls. She seemed fixated on burning things; fire, to her, was the ultimate weapon of destruction, just as her religion taught that sinners would be cast into a lake to suffer hellfire and damnation. Neither Charles nor I could find a valid rationale for this kind of action, so we didn't even try to understand it. But this was the type of religious upbringing that *all* her children rebelled against after leaving home.

Tender Years

There was a phonograph record my kindergarten teacher at Lincoln Elementary, Ms. Stella Broholm, played for our class, a classic titled "Amaryllis," although I don't remember the name of the composer. How I loved that song, so much so that I picked it out on the classroom piano. Ms. Broholm heard me, and the next thing I knew, she had sent a note to Mother asking her to come over to the classroom. When Mother arrived, Ms. Broholm asked me to play the song, which, little showoff that I was, I gladly did. By then I had also figured out the left-hand part, so I wasn't playing only the melody. When I finished, Ms. Broholm turned to Mother and exclaimed, "Mrs. Gordon, Shirley is playing that piece in the exact same key and just like the music is written. I really think she should have piano lessons!"

The year was 1934, right in the middle of the Depression. I know Mother's first thought had to be regarding money. Daddy had taken a pay cut at the Y because of the Depression, so he was only making fifteen dollars a week. A part-time job at a gas station yielded him an additional ten dollars weekly. His earnings had to cover not only the thirty-dollar-per-month payments on the house but also food and clothing for seven people. Where on earth would he find money for something as seemingly nonessential as piano lessons for me? Accordingly, I put it out of my mind.

We had a rather beat-up old piano at home on which all of us banged, playing the usual kid stuff like "Chopsticks" and "Papa, Papa, Have You Heard?" Next year in the first grade my teacher, Ms.

Hattie Harp, asked the class if any of us played a musical instrument, and I enthusiastically raised my hand and said, "I can play the piano!"

You know it was Charles who saw me from his classroom seat as Ms. Harp led me to a piano out in the hall, and he who heard the vibrant strains of "Chopsticks" fill the air. Ms. Harp's face turned beet-red as she led me back down the hall, saying only that "Chopsticks" wasn't quite what she had in mind. I was chagrined and crushed—even more so when Charles regaled the family at dinnertime by telling of my exploit and of his embarrassment at my performance. The jig was up; I then had to tell what had transpired, reiterating my claim of being able to play the piano. It hadn't occurred to me to play "Amaryllis" instead.

I also remember Ms. Harp as quite possibly having saved my life when I was in her class. A little boy named Jimmy, who liked me, was having a birthday party, and his father sent the invitations to Ms. Harp to pass out. Jimmy's parents had just undergone a divorce, an uncommon occurrence back then, so his father was giving the party for him. When Ms. Harp handed me the invitation, she told me it was a note to my mother telling her what a naughty girl I had been. I believed her, stuck the note in my purse, and didn't even think of passing it on to Mother.

In the meantime, it seems none of the kids showed up at the party, and Jimmy's father was so depressed and despondent that later that same evening he poisoned the ice cream, fed some to Jimmy, and committed suicide by eating some himself. It was quite a traumatic experience for Jimmy's classmates.

A few weeks later Mother glanced through my purse, saw an envelope addressed to her, and proceeded to open and read it. It was the invitation to Jimmy's party. Mother said she would have let me go; I don't know if my attendance would have changed the course of events at all, or perhaps I too would have been a victim. But I only felt a sense of relief that I had *not* gone. If Ms. Harp had said the note was telling Mother what a good girl I had been, I would have given it to her immediately.

Now for some good news: I finally started formal piano lessons when I was three months shy of turning eight. Since I had to practice an hour every day, Mother said I didn't have to help with washing the dishes anymore; the boys would do them. There was quite a bit of grumbling from Charles—"Hey, doing dishes is *girls'* work!"

He hadn't heard the worst yet. Added to the ignominy of doing dishes was the fact that Daddy couldn't afford the weekly $1.50 cost, so on Sunday afternoons the entire family went to my teacher's studio and cleaned it in exchange for my lessons. This caused even more ill feeling and grumbling on the boys' part, for while the others busily wielded dust cloths, brooms, and mops, I was practicing in the back studio.

Charles waxed quite voluble on the subject: "Hey, you're getting off easy—*we* have to do all the work and we're missing some of our favorite radio programs, all because of you!" Why he thought practicing wasn't work I don't know, for there were interminable scales, technique, harmony, and theory to be learned, as well as memorization to be accomplished. The latter was especially important because my teacher would not allow any of her pupils to set music up in front of them at recital time; everything must be performed from memory. I knew only that "Practice!" was Mother's dictum, so practice I did. I could do nothing carelessly, for even from the other studio Mother was listening to my playing, and if she thought I was practicing in the least hint of a lackadaisical manner she would come running in to pull my hair and slap me.

Ms. Mary Elizabeth Miller, my teacher, had the major portion of the studio, which was located on the second floor of a building up on High Street; a Kohler Plumbing store occupied the ground floor. Even with two Steinway concert grands and a couple of Steinway uprights, there was still ample room for the studio to serve as a concert and recital hall. Mrs. Clara Ellfeldt Kantzler, my teacher's friend and a fellow graduate of the University of Leipzig in Germany, taught from the rear studio, and it too was included in our Sunday cleaning. I think they really got their $1.50 worth.

Ms. Miller was a snowy-haired, soft-spoken perfectionist who would accept nothing less than a student's best capability. Kind and gentle, she could become a raging tyrant if, during a lesson, she thought you were not putting forth your best effort. After graduating with a degree in music, Ms. Miller had come to this country, teaching at the American Conservatory of Music in Chicago before settling on a small farm in Shipshewana, Indiana, a Mennonite enclave. She was reputed to be Elkhart's finest private teacher, and Daddy said if I was going to study, it should be with the best. Other teachers in Elkhart charged between twenty-five and fifty cents per lesson. The fact that Ms. Miller asked for and received $1.50 speaks for itself, and her students were drawn from the most affluent people in town—except for me!

Shortly after I began lessons, several of the other pupils' mothers advised Ms. Miller that they didn't want their daughters taking piano lessons from the same teacher as that Shirley Gordon, who was, after all, a little colored girl. Mother and I fully expected her to say that she wouldn't be able to continue teaching me, but she fooled both Mother and me and those pupils' mothers by refusing to turn me away.

She was able to turn the prejudices of those small-town people into a great source of motivation for me: I would *show* them better than I ever could tell them that race, ethnic background, or outward appearance had nothing to do with inner talent, latent ability, and a determination to succeed. It was a matter of having the right instructor to develop it all. Naturally, Mother was right beside me, urging me to give it my all, to be the best and thereby make her and Daddy proud of me. My failure would also be theirs.

And Mother made sure that each spring at recital time, I had just as pretty a new dress and shoes as did the other students—

whose parents, I am sure, were a lot more affluent than the Gordons. She considered this her contribution to my success; the rest was up to me. A portrait of Leah and me [see "Sisters" on page 147] shows the typical outfits she bought for us. I never thought to inquire how or where she got the money for these lovely clothes, but I also knew she would not let the white students outshine *her* daughter.

In May of 1940, Ms. Miller presented me in a solo recital. You can see how I must have worked in those twenty months of lessons, for my program was entirely classical: Schumann, Bach, Mozart, and Beethoven, all performed from memory. We had decided there would be four groups of three selections each, with an intermission after the second group, for a total of twelve pieces plus two selections played for encores. I have always regretted not having a printed program, which would have made a memorable keepsake, but I do have my memories. That is something that no one, anywhere, can ever take away from me.

For my recital, the wife of the editor of the local newspaper, the *Elkhart Truth,* made a special trip to Chicago to purchase the material for the yellow organdy gown Mother made for me. A tiny white print floated into the fabric, and the square neckline was set off at each corner with a small white satin bow. The skirt, with its softly gathered waist, fell to the floor in a full sweep of sunshine-yellow, while the puffed sleeves, also trimmed with white satin bows, gave me an almost angelic appearance. A beautician friend of Mother's washed and set my auburn hair in my usual "Shirley Temple" curls. But when I was dressed, horrors! We had forgotten the organdy was sheer, and you could see right through it. The problem was solved when Mother got out one of *her* under-slips, adjusted the straps, and voila! No more see-through.

The evening went off without a hitch. The other students and their families all came—some, I'm sure, to see the little colored girl fall flat on her face. A newspaper announcement printed a few days before the event brought out a crowd that filled the studio to overflowing, and some people had to stand. Seated in the very front row with Daddy, Leah, all the boys, and my grandparents, Mother was "playing" each selection right along with me as though her sheer force of will would carry me through.

Memory served me well; I didn't forget anything or make a single mistake, and everyone said I played with expression and gusto. It was undoubtedly this recital that made Mother decide I would become a concert pianist. Ms. Miller said that in that case, I should have started lessons no later than age five, so I was behind already and would have to work just that much harder.

Quite naturally Charles had to tease me and call me, variously, "Paderewski" or "Rubenstein," since he didn't know the names of any female concert pianists. I wouldn't have minded in the least if he had called me "Dame Myra Hess." I could tell he was proud of me—even though it meant sharing the spotlight a bit, and he wasn't too keen on that. He still wanted to be the only one of us kids that Mother and Daddy and the public praised. It didn't bother me at all, because he was already making a name for himself in academics, music, and sports. I felt there was room at the top for us both.

Since all of the family was working to make my dream possible, the least I could do was cooperate. Practice sessions were increased to an hour before school and an hour after, plus two hours straight on Sunday, as Ms. Miller began laying the foundation that would help me meet the entrance requirements of any school in the country.

By now I was the pianist for church services, which thrilled Mother to no end, for as she put it, I was able to serve God with my talent. As far as I was concerned, I did it because our tiny church had no one else to play for services, plus Mother said I had to. Ms. Miller said that playing hymns was excellent practice in learning to sight-read music, which must have been true, for I quickly acquired this ability and gained a reputation for being able to read anything set in front of me.

Imagine, if you will, my gratification and pride when, upon finishing the fifth grade, the school principal asked me to play a march for "graduation" exercises. I complied with a truly rousing march. At last, I was able to prove to Ms. Harp that I could play the piano. A photograph of the Lincoln Elementary School band and orchestra, with me seated behind the big bass drum, was taken for the *Elkhart Truth* newspaper, and it is a picture I will always treasure.

Well, it had been an eventful year for me, that year when I was ten. In addition to the recital—which, of course, was the high point of my year—there was the added excitement of finding I would be going directly from the fifth to the seventh grade. I would be in junior high school! My only problem had been with math, which I hated. Ms. Zook, my teacher, told Mother that all my other subjects came easily to me, but math I had to work at, so I had decided I didn't like it. Mother tutored me at home, and I passed the math test with flying colors.

Looking back, I don't understand my dislike for math, since I loved everything else that involved precision: music and tempo, rules for English, historical dates and facts. If someone told me when to add, subtract, multiply, or divide, I could do it easily, but if I had to figure out the steps for myself, I folded. To me, story problems were just so many sad tales.

That same year, all five of us kids were baptized into Mother's church. It was something she wanted us to do, and we didn't dare gainsay her. In hindsight, I feel none of us genuinely realized exactly what we were doing, not in those tender years. Our mindset may also have been influenced by the "clean black" syndrome with which we'd all been brainwashed, together with Mother's apocalyptic view of cause and effect: do this and live, do that and die. This probably made stronger persons of us, with higher ideals, principles, and aspirations than we might otherwise have had. But to us, that religion seemed to be filled with too many restrictions: you *can't* do this, you *can't* do that, with not enough *can do.*

I think we all submitted to this baptism believing it would assure us of Mother's love forever so that she would never abandon us. However, it didn't prevent her from threatening to send us to an orphanage upon what seemed to be the slightest provocation. I yearned to find a church that believed in a loving God: a God who loves and cherishes me, a God who knows my weaknesses yet loves and cares for me despite them. It would be many years before I found the loving church and benevolent God I had sought for so long.

During this time in our young lives Mother was definitely in control. Under her threats of abandonment when we did not do exactly as she wished, we would not—could not—disregard her wishes or commands, at least not until we were all grown, had left home, and were living on our own. Her approval meant more to us than any other authority.

We were denied a sense of, or a belief in, our own reality, because the true self can only originate in those earliest relationships, those sensitive attunements between mother and child that are to be nurtured from infancy, then encouraged to grow and blossom. It is so much more than being allowed to think or act on our own. It is fundamental to the mother's role that she should protect a child while it develops that firm belief in its own reality.

Denied this, we wandered for years trying to discover just who, what, and where we were. It certainly led to Charles's lifelong search for a place to be somebody. How very painful it is to endure a lifetime of searching for a place in which you could not only *be* yourself, but also *know* yourself and be someone. We were unable to feel that we were loved for who we were, her children, but only for our achievements and our successes; any good qualities we might possess weren't our own at all, merely inherited from or developed in us by her. Our childhood was sacrificed in our efforts to win that love. We were never able to obtain it from her, and our lives were greatly impoverished and diminished by her denial of our needs.

Teenage Years

I loved the seventh grade at Central Junior High where, like Charles, I was an eager participant in a lot of things. It was so exciting to meet all the other students garnered from the various elementary schools scattered around Elkhart, all of us together in a huge building, with larger classes and the new experience of having a different teacher for each subject. A number of the teachers had taught Mother, and remembering how much they had liked her, they welcomed first Charles and then me with open arms. Not only was I getting good grades (even in algebra!), I was taking part in what were called "extracurricular activities," which I had never dreamed existed. Charles had never told us anything about this. On the staff of the school paper, I started writing poetry like crazy, and better still, they even published some of it!

Study hall was my favorite time for creativity, and the poor teacher assigned as monitor, a Ms. Carnelly, had to suffer through the reading of my literary efforts, mostly poetry and short plays. Like Charles, I loved showing off and being in the limelight, so I made sure she saw everything and would wait by her desk for her comments. I had an intense desire for adult approval, for someone who would say, "Oh, that's very good, Shirley!" It was a whole new stage for me upon which to appear, one in which adults other than my parents expressed approval regarding something I had done. I worked for that pat on the head like an actress working for applause from an audience.

Both Charles and I had been thrust into the spotlight by Mother from the time we were very young, so we were accustomed to it and, in fact, thrived on it. Our deep desire for approval and personal credit, no matter who offered it, drove us to do our absolute best lest we shame or disgrace Mother with a poor public performance. We were always *on*.

Elkhart High's 1941–42 yearbook reports that the choir took first division honors at a state contest in Butler, Indiana. Charles, framed by choir director Richard Herzig and his baton, is on the second row from top. Charles went on in the 1942–43 school year to sing with the a cappella choir under the direction of William Gowdy. Used by permission of the Elkhart Community Schools.

High school college career day, Charles, *seated second from right, front row,* 1944, high school yearbook. Used by permission of Elkhart Community Schools.

With the increased audience we had an expanded opportunity to shine, and Charles strode across this new stage in his seven-league boots while I toddled after him in my two-leaguers. Though Mother still directed us, still controlled us, we had a fresh audience to tell us how good we were, and we reveled in it. Admiration, praise, and recognition from others gave us, we thought, star status, and we began to think we really had something worthwhile to offer the world. We were determined to pick up the gauntlet Mother had flung down before us, to obey her command to "grow up and be *somebody*; make me proud of you!" These goals were also prompted by an inner spirit that guided the things we chose to do, for we were never content to stay in the background.

While Stanley, the shy brother, did seem content to remain in the shadows, Cecil tried to get the attention *he* craved by bragging about his siblings; being neither a scholar nor a musician, the preferred coin of Gordon values, he made his bid for attention and approval in the only acceptable way he could.

Leah was still too young to know what she wanted to do in life. She was resentful because the only attention she was getting at home was through being chastised, both physically and mentally. Mother and Daddy were determined to force her to obey according to their will. I give her credit for having the courage and strength to deny them the power to break her spirit, for they succeeded only in bending her will to theirs during the years she remained at home.

Leah threw away the opportunity for a music scholarship on the cello at Oberlin College and consorted with the lowest elements of life in Elkhart—being promiscuous, hanging out with the wrong people, drinking—you name it, she did it. Even the fact that she played cello in the high school orchestra meant little to her. She wanted to quit high school, but they did manage to cajole her into at least getting her diploma. After that, she took off on a downward path, never looking back, and I only hope her defiance proved itself worth it in the long run.

Elkhart High's 1943–44 yearbook lists a the one-act play *No Greater Love* as the Senior Dramatics Club's contribution to a January 21 entertainment evening. In the club photo *(top)*, Charles is on the top row, at center. In the photo *(bottom)*, originally captioned "Explaining our angle to Supt. Church," Charles is at far right. Used by permission of the Elkhart Community Schools.

After she left home, she did exactly as she pleased, even though a lot of things were beyond any of our comprehension as to *why* she did them. I believe she won the final battle by defying them again and again for the rest of her life, although she shortened that life by so doing. She kept her vow to them, as if she was saying, "You are determined to make me be *somebody* just to reflect glory on you and have people tell you what wonderful parents you are. Well, I'm just as determined you aren't going to do it; I'm going to be just what I want to be, which is *nothing!*"

She was a driven spirit, and I believe it all started with the harsh treatment she both observed and received as a child. She, like Stanley, had suffered physical and mental abuse, but she was never able to overcome her anguish.

Girl Reserves

There was a girls' club called Girl Reserves (later changed to Y-Teens), which I was eligible to join in the seventh grade. It met at and was sponsored by the YWCA up on Lexington, the same place Daddy had worked for years as the maintenance man. The main purposes of the group were to foster world fellowship, learn about health, and to perform service work for those less fortunate. Some of the girls had been my elementary-school classmates, so I felt quite at ease and comfortable among them and enjoyed the new experience of being part of a larger group interested in clean living.

Some weeks after we began meeting, several mothers phoned the Y's executive director and complained about their letting a colored girl be in a club with their little white girls. They couldn't understand why I didn't attend Girl Reserves meetings with the other colored girls at the Booker T. Washington Community Center, across the tracks on the South Side. While I was acquainted with a few of those girls, none lived close to me; we had gone to different elementary schools and different churches, so we had different circles of friends. I thought the girls I had known at Lincoln Elementary were old friends. Whoever the mothers were that complained, they certainly didn't do it face-to-face, evidently preferring the anonymity of the telephone.

That summer most of the girls were making plans to go to Camp Kil-O-Qua (an Indian name meaning "Lake of the Great Star") for a week or two, where we would participate in land and water sports, studies of nature, and arts and crafts—all activities that were especially appealing to me. How excited I was, for Mother and Daddy had given me permission to attend. This would be my first overnight trip away from home without family members.

Daddy always drove the official YWCA car, a 1934 Plymouth loaded to capacity with the girls' luggage. Mother had bought me new summer play clothes, and I was ready with my little bag packed when the word came down: there were separate dates for the camp—one week for the white girls, another for the colored. If I went, they insisted I would have to attend the camp for the colored girls.

Mother and Daddy asked for an exception for me on the grounds that all my friends, the girls I had grown up with and knew so well, were attending the white girls' camp. Since Daddy worked at the Y and the entire executive board knew our family well, my parents felt their request would be granted.

It was denied, and needless to say, I was extremely hurt and disappointed. Why could these people not have had the courage of their convictions, as my piano teacher had, and made a positive stand on my behalf? Wouldn't it have been more in keeping with the ideals of the YWCA? This was another example of the "white mask, black world" syndrome we would repeatedly meet throughout our lives in Elkhart.

One of Charles's former classmates recalled this incident in a recent letter to me, although more than fifty years had passed. She had been both horrified and embarrassed at the Y's decision, which she knew about because her mother was on the board and had voted for the denial. This woman said she never quite forgave her mother for this, because it didn't seem Christian-like to her, as well as very much in opposition to what the Young Women's Christian Association stood for. She also wanted to express her feelings of respect and admiration for our family because of what she termed the "dignified way" we handled the situation.

Thinking back to those years, I have to remember that in the 1930s in that prejudiced small town, even though my skin was as light as theirs, they categorized me as a colored girl: talented, yes; smart, yes; but *still* colored and not to be accepted as one of them. I wasn't trying to be white; I was simply trying to participate in and make a contribution to something I believed was worthwhile. After all, hadn't Mother and Daddy always told us that color didn't count, that it was what you had in your heart and head that was important? In the final analysis, color mattered more than anything else.

What hurt the most was that the rejection of my parents' request was passed on to Daddy by the very same women who, over the years, had given so many lovely toys, books, and articles of clothing to both Leah and me when their daughters had outgrown them. That really stung, even though their generosity had often led Daddy to often make another of his favorite remarks: "You kids have things that few white kids do, and no niggers have 'em at all!" I can remember thinking on one occasion, "Maybe that's true, but *you* didn't provide them; the white folks did!"

My childhood was greatly enriched by their generosity, for it was through them I first discovered that the world of books was a magic carpet for my mind, a world I could enter any time I opened a book, to soar away to an entirely different time and place. Even though the givers have long been gone, I will always remember that through them, my spirit was fed. Love of books and literature is a gift no one can ever erase from my heart.

News clipping documenting segregated facilities at the YWCA, printed in 1948 (reprinted in 1976) by *The Truth* newspaper for the U.S. bicentennial celebration. Copyrighted material used by permission of *The Truth*.

> *In 1948:* "Lincoln School (on Oakland) is having a Halloween party tonight under sponsorship of the city recreation department, PTAs and city schools. All city grade schools will have parties tonight. The Y-Teens' party for senior high school students will be at the YWCA (West Lexington); the junior high schools pupils at the YMCA (West Franklin) and the Negro children at Booker T. Washington center (800 block of South Sixth Street)."

We were also advised that Daddy's job would be at risk if we protested publicly over the decision, and, of course, his work was more important than my feelings. So I dropped out of Girl Reserves and forgot all about having once dreamed of going to camp.

Living the American dream of freedom and equality for all hadn't penetrated the hearts and minds of those WASP mothers, nor those in executive positions at the Y; instead, they were fiercely determined to maintain the status quo. While the colored girls did have their own separate (but equal) facility and capable directors who offered quite a few activities, there was still no acceptance in the main YWCA for colored people, Catholics, Jews, Mormons, or immigrants. I was totally unaware of all this back in the early 1940s.

In my small church—which had a membership of only eighteen to twenty people, mostly adults—there was little opportunity for a social life, although we did have a youth group called Missionary Volunteers, which would have been comparable to the Girl or Boy Scouts out in the world. Besides, a good number of the South Side girls' meetings and activities occurred on Friday nights or Saturdays, which would have been against our religious observance of the Sabbath. For the Gordon kids, everything was based on strict religious obedience; our religion believed in staying separate from the world—which created in us a deep-seated, yet hidden, yearning for acceptance by the world.

It came as a big surprise, although it shouldn't have, when, during my senior year as I was getting ready to attend college on the near North Side of Chicago, my application for a room at the YWCA nearest my school (since my college had no dormitory of its own) was refused. My references were from the women in charge of Elkhart's Y. My request was turned down because, they quite candidly informed me, they didn't have facilities to accommodate colored girls, suggesting that I instead apply at the Phyllis Wheatley YWCA branch on Chicago's South Side, which was totally segregated. This branch was quite a distance from my school and in the opposite direction, so living there would have entailed at least an hour-and-a-half ride on the streetcar. In my naivete, I had thought all we had to do was be able to pay the room rent; my scholarship paid all my other expenses. Instead, they wanted me to live in segregated conditions, something totally alien to my childhood environment and experience, at least as far as the Gordons were concerned.

I ended up in a privately owned and operated women's dormitory, totally segregated but only half an hour from my school, one recommended and thoroughly checked out by Cousin Ora as being of good repute. There was never any problem with my following their rules, for I had been following rules all my life. They made accommodations for me to have a desk for doing my homework, since quite a few of the young women who lived there were working and not in school. I was very happy there, got along well with all the girls, and came to the conclusion that the Young Women's Christian Association did not live up to its name. While their women may have been young, the Christian part seemed totally lacking to me, and I never again approached anyone connected to it.

It was beyond my comprehension how Mother could, in light of all this, bring herself to serve as a president of the YWCA in later years. I heard their policy had changed from strict segregation—with the colored girls only attending meetings and participating in activities held at the Community Center in the heart of the South Side—to a mixed membership. I never tried to find out if this was so. At any rate, I graduated from Elkhart High School in June 1947, and I know the YWCA's Girl Reserves was still segregated in 1948. Separate but equal?

Sports Star

When Charles wanted to join the Fighting Fifty, a high school sports club, some white parents tried vigorously to keep him out. But eligibility was based on athletic ability and acceptance by his fellow students, so he became the first black student ever invited to join that fraternity-type club. After all, hadn't he set a high-jump record in a state contest that stood for a number of years? Had he not participated in and won numerous first and second places in various athletic contests, both locally and on a statewide basis?

Still, no one knew his hurt or frustration over the fact that at state track meets he had to stay on the bus or wait in the private cars carrying some of the athletes while the coach and the white athletes went into a restaurant to eat on the way home. Food was brought out to him, for restaurants wouldn't serve a colored person. He later told me that he felt as though he wasn't even considered human, for through a window on one occasion he saw a dog eating from a plate on the restaurant's floor, and some patrons even stopped to pat the animal on the head—yet *he* couldn't even go inside. He reconciled these feelings by telling himself that the adults responsible for those slights didn't know *him*, and he refused to take it personally.

[facing page] "Harriers Rate High in Conference Action." According to Elkhart High's 1942–43 yearbook, the Harriers' cross-country team "finished the season with a much better win average than that of losses." In the Northern Indiana High Conference Meet at Erskine Country Club, "Elkhart placed fourth in a field of ten teams." Charles was team captain and first among the most consistent scorers. "Captain Gordon led Elkhart scoring by pacing the Streaks in most of the meets." *(top)* Coach Chelsea Boone checks season points with Captain Gordon. *(middle)*, originally captioned "Getting into their stride," Charles runs second from left. *(bottom)* Coach (*left*) and captain (*right*) bracket a few team members. Used by permission of Elkhart Community Schools.

Camille, *center front*, was captain of Roosevelt Junior High's 1920 basketball team.

ELKHART

A track star, he was also captain of the track team, jumped the hurdles, was on the relay and cross-country teams, and won numerous school letters, which were awarded only to those who were outstanding in their achievements. In fact, he won more letters than he had sweaters on which to affix them: a total of sixteen! It was not without justification that his nickname was "Flash" Gordon. But all these things didn't matter to the outside world; to them he was still just a colored boy.

The most difficult thing for Charles to accept was that while he was a star on the athletic field, once the competitions were ended, his fellow athletes slapped him on the back and congratulated him, then abruptly left him standing alone while they went off to party and celebrate together. "Why," he wondered, "can't they see how much it would mean to me to be asked to join them?"

He was expected to socialize only with people of color. And the problem was, he didn't know how people really felt toward him and his achievements. All his associates were white; he lived in and grew up in a white neighborhood; all the clubs he belonged to were composed of white members; his classmates were all white; and his parents were constantly encouraging him to be as "white" in his thinking and acting as possible. Again, their preachings and teachings that color didn't matter seemed to him to be the height of ignorance, posturing, and denial, and he grew to deeply doubt the veracity of their statements.

The only contact he had with other colored boys consisted of hearing their snide remarks at some local athletic events, spoken loudly enough to be overheard, about "niggers tryin' to be white, and thinkin' they *are* white," which made him extremely uncomfortable and ill at ease on the rare occasions he was around them. Nor did it help matters that the white boys at school, while accepting his many accomplishments, didn't try to include him in their social life. They didn't "hang out" together up on Main Street at the local Walgreens drugstore, and he had no "best buddy" to talk to. I don't believe he was ever invited to one of their homes; all contact was carried on at the school and related facilities. In the long run, there was a Mason-Dixon Line that, in those days, he could never cross.

Jim Brown, the noted football player, once commented on this same phenomenon: "Don't expect to be accepted as one of 'them' on a personal or social basis. You may be cheered on while you're out on the field, and give your all for the school, but once that game is over, you'll find that to them you're still just a colored boy."

This continued Charles's education in the "white mask, black world" phenomenon. By definition: you can present ever so "white" a face (and we are not talking skin color here!) in your thoughts and your actions, but to white people it *is* just a mask, a pretense on your part, for to them, you can never escape your black world. You can never be completely like them; there will always be those genes, that DNA, eternally dividing and separating you—and to them, *theirs* is infinitely better! As a result of being isolated from both white and black worlds, Charles became a loner. It took years of living before he could accept himself *for* himself, and find his own place to be someone.

First Love

Daddy's nine o'clock curfew wreaked havoc with Charles during his senior year in high school, for that was the year he fell in love.

I can understand Daddy's logic: according to our religion we didn't attend social or school functions on Friday nights, not even on Saturday night until after sundown. We didn't attend the movies and we didn't dance, so there was no reason to be out any later. Nine o'clock signaled: "All who are in, stay in; all who are out, stay out, 'cause that door will be *locked*." But Charles was tired of having to convince Cecil and Stanley that it was their duty as brothers to let him in through the upstairs bedroom window after hours. They, in turn, knew they would be severely punished if their part in that operation were ever discovered by Daddy. As aware as he was of everything going on with us kids, he never caught on as to what was happening right under his nose.

But to a red-blooded young man, those restrictions had become untenable; he had to have some space, the chance to make his own decisions, and a modicum of freedom to act on them. A lot of club meetings and practice sessions, both vocal and athletic, went on after school. And on Saturdays there were major events taking place both in and out of town, events that he had trained and practiced for. Letting the team and the school down by missing them was not something he was prepared to do. Most of all, if he never *did* anything, how could he make Mother proud of him, or get to where he could conceivably be "somebody"?

It was then that Charles decided to go live at our grandparents' home. He knew they would not be the jailers Mother and Daddy had been, and he would finally be free to come and go as he wished. Mother raised a big ruckus over this; as usual, her concern was that people would be critical of her and Daddy. Our grandparents stuck up for Charles, insisting he was no longer a little boy and that he deserved the opportunity to use his abilities in the ways for which he had been training all of his young life. Naturally, Mother took it as a personal affront, but his mind was made up. He felt he had been restricted long enough in an effort to make her happy; now it was *his* turn to stretch his wings and fly, to see in which direction his abilities would take him.

Charles was, in truth, the "fair-haired black boy" of the school, taking part in activities that few others of his race had engaged in before. If you covered up his picture in the class of 1944 high school yearbook, the Pennant Annual, and didn't know his ethnic background, a read-through of his accomplishments would be the same as—and in many instances more extensive than—those of the sons

Charles, 1941–42, high school yearbook. Used by permission of Elkhart Community Schools.

and daughters of Elkhart's more affluent and prominent citizens: HI-Y, Dramatics Club, Yell Club, Annual Ad Staff, Student Council, Choir (president), Cross-Country (captain), Track (captain), Boys' Glee Club, Tumbling Team, Blue Jackets, Superintendent's Council. He was also the featured tenor soloist with the high school choir, winning numerous vocal contests and invited to appear on many programs around town.

A prediction of his future, Charles's membership in the Dramatics Club gave him his first true taste of the satisfactions of performing on the boards and, in turn, led to his later involvement with the movies, stage, and theater as an actor, producer, and director. He was elated to find that a role on stage enabled him to be somebody else altogether. It didn't matter behind those white floodlights whether he was colored, white, or a member of any other ethnic group; he could *become* the character he was portraying. This opened up an entirely new world for him, one that was quite satisfying. Writing for the school newspaper and the annual *Threshold Magazine* also gave him his first insight into writing, and there too he could become one with whatever characters he set down on paper.

When Charles discovered the delights of feminine companionship and had the "nerve" to fall in love with a white girl who also sang in the choir, her mother was absolutely outraged. How dare a "nigger" presume to be in love with *her* daughter? That was okay with our mother; for once in her life she was glad that prejudice entered the picture, for she considered the girl and her family "poor white trash" and would have been devastated if anything serious had developed from their relationship. She was evidently as racially biased in *her* thinking as were the girl's mother and other whites in the town.

To Charles, it seemed only natural that the two of them were attracted to each other. She too was a member of the choir, with a lyric soprano voice that soared heart-stoppingly. Blonde and blue-eyed, she combined a knockout figure with a bubbly personality. They were in daily contact, since a quartet had been formed with her as the soprano, an attractive dark-haired girl (who later went on to join the Phil Spitalny All-Women's Choir) singing contralto, Charles the tenor, and a tall young man who sang bass. Propinquity, that old "bugaboo" of the white race, was working overtime, as were their emerging hormones. Continually placed in close proximity to each other and finding a shared love and enjoyment of music, they became even closer. Charles felt he had much more in common with her than any girl he had ever met.

Some of the Kiwanis Club members protested the pairing of Charles and this girl in duets and as part of the aforementioned quartet, becoming quite vocal in their protests to the choir director. As a result Charles became quite embittered against that organization for a long time, to the extent that he never wanted to sing for them again.

Their involvement on a personal basis escalated rapidly as the result of their need to hide their growing friendship from the outside world, for in Elkhart there was no place a colored boy and a white girl could go for a date. They would both have been ostracized, perhaps worse, had their feelings been publicly revealed. As a result, they ended up spending a lot of time together at her apartment during the hours her mother was at work.

One night her mother came home earlier than expected, and all hell broke loose. The girl was packed up and sent out of town, without even a chance to say good-bye. Although Charles never heard from or saw her again, he never forgot her, and the sadness lingered for many years. He wondered again, "What is so 'bad' about being 'colored'? Why do white people hate us so? My skin color doesn't make me less a person than I have always been!"

Throughout his life, Charles recalled this girl as his first true love, and he would use their involvement as a composite model for the character of Maxine in *No Place to Be Somebody.* Even though they never met again, I thought the similarities in their later years were quite uncanny. Unbeknownst to each other, both ended up in

Texas, that refuge state for seekers, actually living just a few hours' drive apart. He outlived her by a mere four months; both elected to be cremated; both wanted to stay at home in Texas—her ashes were interred in Austin, while his were scattered along the Canadian River Breaks in the Texas Panhandle. While they had both married other people and led widely divergent lives, in the end Texas had become for them a place of refuge and healing, a place of freedom to be themselves—and above all, a place where they could, like other Texans before them, feel they had arrived home at last.

Some people seem destined never to realize any one of these circumstances or conditions; they were indeed fortunate to find all of them.

"Beethoven"

Young as we were, for all our lives up to this point Mother had selected and pursued her own dreams of perfection and public recognition in Charles and myself. I failed to understand why Stanley, Cecil, and Leah weren't facing the same demands that were made on the two of us. The pressures we were undergoing were starting to play havoc with my mental state, haunting both my days and my nights. Urged always to "transcend," it was beginning to have an effect on us.

Being the younger of the two, I was perhaps suffering more than Charles was at that time and place. Another reason might have been that since I was a girl, I was more closely supervised by Mother. As a boy, Charles at fourteen was able to escape some of her dominance by simply not being present. He was finding a refuge by being physically active in sports, which got him out of the house, whereas I was trapped inside the limitations imposed upon me by being female, the elder daughter, and expected to be around Mother constantly.

She demanded that I confide in her all my thoughts, my dreams, my aspirations. Thinking that it made me a "good" daughter, I complied with her wishes; seemingly I had no other choice.

Checking my thesaurus, I find that some synonyms for *transcend* are "to be greater or better than, pass, exceed, top, better, overshadow, outdo, surpass, best, eclipse, excel, outstrip, outshine." It also means to be accepted or approved, to be greater or better than, to go through life in a certain way.

All of the foregoing describes perfectly what we had to endure, starting with Mother and Daddy, then in competition first with our siblings, next our schoolmates, and finally out in the world. We were given no margin for error. The die had been cast by Mother, and the pressure was omnipresent to "transcend" being colored, which Mother insisted we had to do to prove all the other points. What tremendous physical and mental erosion this inevitably caused, for Mother was intransigent in that regard, maintaining constantly that *we* had the power to overcome resistance wherever, whenever, and however it manifested itself.

For me, there seemed to be no avenue of escape from this buildup of pressure. I had an intuitive feeling, a beginning dread that somewhere, sometime, the bottom would drop out of everything, for no one can be as perfect all the time as she insisted and demanded that we be. Filled with a deep foreboding, I lacked any clue as to what I could do to prevent it, yet this expectation of doom made me feel powerless to avoid a disaster, whatever form or shape it took. Forewarned was not forearmed for me.

It was an ironic twist of fate that kept me from attending that YWCA camp the summer I was eleven, for it was during the exact same time I would have been away from home that my life changed forever. I have often wondered if the stress and strain I had been under after the YWCA's denial had been the "straw that broke the camel's back," releasing such a floodgate of emotions that I could only *react* and not *act*, and thereby my life was forever altered.

On one particular summer afternoon the azure sky had been cloudless while a gentle breeze wafted across the front porch, where Mother had let me have a tea party with cookies and lemonade as a special treat to share with a friend of mine, Charlene Kendall, whose friendship with our family dated from the days on Hudson Street when we had been neighbors.

A perky child with dimples that showed whenever she smiled, which was often, Charlene had previously introduced me to some of the finer points of baton twirling, even going so far as to loan me her baton *and* a brief red-satin, flare-skirted costume, which I put on and pranced around the backyard, practicing. (Mother would never have let me wear such a short skirt in public: it wasn't modest!) I thought I looked very cute in this outfit and was engrossed in learning this skill—probably seeking a new way to be in the spotlight, for have you ever seen a baton twirler anyplace other than at the front of a parade or leading a band?

This particular day Mother had let me set up our small red table with folding chairs out on the front porch, where we gobbled up the goodies in very short order. Eventually Charlene left to go home, while I put everything away. About half an hour later I began to feel lightheaded and dizzy. Mother, who was outdoors helping Daddy water the garden, called out to Cecil and me to put fresh linen on the beds, since she had removed the sheets earlier to launder them. Instead I went inside and lay down on the sofa for a moment, trying to calm my spinning head.

Cecil, thinking I was trying to get out of doing some work, went out and told Mother, "Hey, Mother, Shirley ain't helping, she's in there laying down!" She knew this was quite unlike her usually obedient daughter and came in to find out what the trouble was.

When I explained how I felt, she told me to stay on the sofa while she helped Cecil, and then I could get in bed. This sounded wonderful to me. I had never in my life felt even the least bit sick and gone to bed without awakening the next morning feeling just fine. This time, I was certain it would be the same. Before long, Cecil came downstairs to tell me Mother said my bed was ready . . . and I couldn't hear or understand a word he was saying!

The next morning Mother let me sleep a bit later. When I awoke, sunlight was streaming through the crisp white curtains and reflecting off the walls. I stretched lazily, for sleeping late was uncommon in the Gordon household, and thought, "Yes! I feel great! I'm not dizzy anymore!" I lay there for a few moments longer, simply enjoying the peace and quiet. I didn't hear my brothers or my sister making any noise; there was absolute silence. I glanced idly through my bedroom door, across the hall and out through my parents' bedroom window, and what I saw sent me screaming and running downstairs to Mother. A freight train was going by, and while I could feel some vibration, *I couldn't hear it.*

Thus began what Charles called "Shirley's Beethoven period." He claimed I was only pretending to be deaf because I admired Beethoven so much and was trying to imitate him; he finally stopped this teasing when he saw the paroxysm of tears it caused. I couldn't differentiate tones on the piano, and I couldn't hear or understand words in normal conversation. To communicate with me at all, Mother had to use a pencil and paper: "You know, if you truly are deaf, we'll have to see about sending you away to a special school."

All my life I'd fought, as had my siblings, against her threats of abandonment; was I now fated to be the one who abandoned *them* by having to go away, to live separate and apart from them? Were the years of obedience, of caring, of making myself into the kind of child I believed my parents wanted—no, make that *demanded*—to go for naught?

This deafness became the physical manifestation of a deep-seated, secret desire to escape from my surroundings, a seeking for a sense of my own reality. I had learned at a tender age that I could escape to another world by reading voraciously, in an intense absorption in my music, or through all my different games of pretend.

Most of all I wanted *not* to hear the verbal abuse directed at Leah and Stanley. Now I discovered I no longer had the need to bring my joke book to the dinner table to put Daddy in a good mood, for I had discovered the ultimate escape. All my other efforts had not won me unconditional love or a sense of my own reality, but being unable to hear what was taking place around me enabled me to deny that those things were real. From that day forward, none of this chaos could ever again shrivel my ears or my soul, and before long I felt a lessening of the absolute control exercised by Mother.

I was still physically in their world, but no longer *of* their world. I could retreat into *my* own world at will by closing them out either entirely or partially, depending on what was going on around me. I knew a lot of battles still lay ahead in learning to cope with my deafness, but now the ability to escape outweighed all other factors. But what I failed to realize was that my hearing could not be turned on and off like a faucet; now that it was off, who could turn it back on for me?

And so the testing began. The first tests were conducted by our family doctor and friend, Dr. David Todd. Dr. Todd gave me a complete physical, including blood tests and a spinal tap. You can imagine how huge that spinal tap needle looked and felt to an eleven-year-old! I was proud of my ability to withstand the pain of all those needles in my arm and in my back; Dr. Todd told Mother he had adult patients who couldn't have held that still. But he was unable to find any cause for my hearing loss.

I underwent complete audiological testing by Dr. Dale Swihart, Elkhart's leading ear, nose, and throat specialist, who took us into his office on a Sunday afternoon so others wouldn't know he had accepted a colored patient. I do, however, give him and Dr. Todd full credit for making all the necessary arrangements for me to be examined at the University of Michigan Hospital in Ann Arbor, where yet again I underwent the same battery of tests.

With the tests completed and all the results reported, the only thing the doctors could tell Mother was that they could find no medical reason for my hearing loss, and they concluded I had nerve deafness. They recommended that I be fitted for a hearing aid, which I would have to wear for the rest of my life. I panicked: "But I'm only *eleven* years old! Only *old* people have to wear hearing aids!"

What was I going to do? School was scheduled to start in a few weeks. Seventh grade had been pure joy, but now? *But now?* Determinedly, I gritted my teeth and, through painful trial and error, began to teach myself how to read lips and people's facial expressions, even how to interpret body language. I'd had some practice in reading faces by watching Daddy at mealtimes, but my world now encompassed a much larger group of people. There are many letters and words that sound very similar and are formed by the lips in much the same way, and of course people don't move their lips and mouths in exactly the same way. I also found some people, particularly Southerners, who didn't put endings on their words, dropping r's, t's, and g's. And, oh! The things I missed while trying to teach myself through those days of trial and error! I was under stress every waking moment of my life in my efforts to let nothing escape me. My only relief occurred in my dreams at night, where strangely my hearing was always perfect.

Every time I entered a room I felt people were talking about me—which, I later learned, is a common fallacious belief of deaf people. When school started, I had to make sure my seat was immediately in front of the teacher's desk so I could read her lips and face and understand the questions. Some of the teachers had very little patience with my stumbling efforts to understand what was going on, although I admit I delayed telling any of them about my deafness until it became absolutely unavoidable. A lot of my classmates' responses to questions were eternally lost to me; since I didn't know who was answering, I couldn't turn to them in time to read their lips. This meant I had to study even more carefully, memorizing all the correct questions and answers for exams.

The biggest challenge for me was accepting that this deafness was not going to magically disappear and thereby set my world right, as it would have in one of my fairy stories. It was vital for my mindset to be firm so I could work not around but *through* the problem. I discovered very early on that my parents would not let me use my deafness as an excuse for doing less than my best, and since I had opted to remain at home instead of going away to a special school, I had to work within their parameters.

Shortly after I underwent all those tests and we got the results, Mother arranged with the minister who had baptized all five of us children for a special "anointing" of my ears. With utter confidence in him, God, and Mother, I simply *knew* that the next day when I awoke, my hearing would be restored to normal. Well, this did not happen; thus, I had to face spiritual as well as physical disappointment. No longer did I believe in those biblical promises that prayers would be answered if one asked and truly believed. I had a child's faith that I would be healed, and when it didn't occur I literally turned a deaf ear to God.

I could no longer believe in a God who didn't deliver on his promises, so from that time on, I sat in church and read the Psalms and the Song of Solomon as though they were poetry, since I couldn't hear or understand the sermon anyway. I did not want to listen to the platitudes and preachings of Mother's church. (Besides, I thought the Song of Solomon was quite erotic reading, and I enjoyed it!)

Next I became aware of an extreme tinnitus, an ever-present ringing in my ears. I didn't know it then, but I would continue to have it for my lifetime. The only way to cope with that continuous noise is by learning to ignore it, which I am able to do most of the time. After all these years it only registers on my mind when I consciously think of it. A magazine article gave me the needed insight in how to handle this problem, which was something quite simple: you cannot think of two different things at the same time, so when you find yourself with an undesirable thought (or in this case, noise), you should try to deliberately think of something else. It worked then, and still does, at least for me.

Well into the school year, Mother talked to someone in the school system and made arrangements for me to be fitted with a hearing aid. Besides the mold that fitted into my ear, there was a halter-like contraption that fastened around my chest, with a pocket in the middle to hold the aid. Three wires ran from the aid's bottom: one to the earpiece and two that led to double batteries strapped on my upper thigh. I felt everyone saw "three me's" when I wore this apparatus, and I was already self-conscious about my just-beginning-to-develop bust.

Piano lessons continued, but it wasn't long before both my teacher and I began to realize I could no longer differentiate the notes starting two octaves above middle C; they all sounded alike. My hearing loss had occurred in the higher tonal frequencies, which meant no violins or flutes could be heard in the higher values, only in their lower tones. Ms. Miller, however, wouldn't let me give up, insisting that if I memorized the music and mastered the techniques of performance, I would have no problem. Little did she know. Accepting these new limitations was one of the most difficult hurdles for me to overcome; to deny their reality would have been pointless and self-defeating.

At this point I had to start normalizing my life. I wanted to do all the things I had always done and then decide if there were new directions open to me.

Such ordinary things as riding my bike or walking to and from school, which the Gordon kids had always done, became a hazard for me, for I had to pay strict attention when crossing the street. But there were other, simpler things that I greatly missed: the songs of birds, the rustle of breezes through leafy treetops, the sounds of crickets chirping on hot summer evenings. The voices of children playing or calling to one another were also out of my hearing range.

I couldn't even hear a classmate who, seeing me walking up ahead, called out, "Wait up!"—so, unhearing, I kept walking. They began to call me "stuck up" and "snob," and I was too embarrassed to tell them of my problem.

Charles was the first to break the good news to me that I would never have any boyfriends to whisper sweet nothings in my ear, therefore I was doomed to be an old maid wearing glasses *and* a hearing aid. I discovered that it was Mother who had asked Charles to play detective in an effort to determine if I really couldn't hear, knowing I would be entirely truthful and honest with him since we had always had a close relationship. I knew he would never knowingly hurt my feelings.

Later, in my mid-teens, I found the boys did still like me, which was a big boost to my ego. Losing my hearing didn't keep me from having crushes on a number of different boys throughout junior and senior high school, although I never let them know it. After all, they were white and this was just not done!

During the last half of eighth grade, several things occurred that convinced me I was learning to cope with my handicap, encouraging me to try still harder in my efforts to live as normal a life as possible. I still played the piano for church and got a lot of satisfaction from doing that. Then the new high school choir director, Mr. Orlando Lansing Lynn, somehow heard that I played the piano. (I suspect Cecil of this, since he was in Mr. Lynn's music appreciation class, and he still could not refrain from boasting about his brother Charles, the tenor, and his sister Shirley, the pianist.) In need of someone to practice with the high school choir, Mr. Lynn requested and received permission from the school authorities for me to join the choir, which usually wasn't permitted until ninth grade. I gladly gave up study hall; I would do my studying at home.

Thus began one of my most enjoyable school experiences, for I fell in love with the harmonics involved in choral music. Better yet, all I had to do was follow the director's lead. My ability to sight-read came in handy every time the choir started a new piece of music. In fact, around that same time I was becoming quite in demand as an accompanist for both vocal and instrumental soloists, a demand that increased during my remaining school years. To this day I don't know how I was able to accompany people and, even with my great hearing loss, be right in step with them as they performed.

It wasn't long afterward that Mr. Lynn received several phone calls from some of the white mothers, insisting he should be using *their* daughters as accompanists for the choir instead of that little colored girl Shirley Gordon. Mr. Lynn was furious. Word got around that he had told them that when their daughters could follow his direction like Shirley, when they could be depended on for regular attendance at rehearsals like Shirley and sight-read music like Shirley, they might be considered *after* I graduated from high school.

I was granted the signal honor of accompanying Charles for his final tenor solo at the choir's spring concert, in recognition of his musical contribution to the group, just before his graduation with the class of '44. To this day I remember the song he sang: "Home to Thee, Lord," by Steinel (I also still remember all the words and music!), and the standing ovation he received.

For my own final appearance with the choir, the director asked me to play a piano solo in recognition of my years of accompanying the choir. The audience was deeply appreciative of my performance of Beethoven's "Sonata Pathetique." The Gordon kids had done it again! It was a definite fact that music had enriched the lives of not only my family but also those whom our music touched.

Mr. Lynn had a beautiful tenor voice. When he was asked to perform several selections at a Sunday afternoon program for the Women's Business and Professional Association in the YWCA auditorium, Mr. Lynn asked Mother if I could be his accompanist. The women really enjoyed his performance (I think most females have a soft spot for tenors!), and the applause was so great he had to give several encores. Afterward, we sat down to enjoy the tea and refreshments being served.

A few days later, Mother told me that several of the ladies in attendance had phoned her to compliment me on my accompanying and also to tell her how much like a "nice young lady" I had conducted myself. I guess they were surprised to find the little colored girl knew which fork to use! It didn't occur to me until much later that this YWCA was the same place where I had been denied permission to belong to the Girl Reserves or attend summer camp. I had put this totally out of my mind, forgetting the hurt and bewilderment at my treatment by becoming fully engrossed in my studies and my music.

A few months into tenth grade, arrangements were made for me to study lip reading with a special teacher from the public schools. After my first session, which Mother also attended, the instructor informed us that I was already a better lip reader than *she* was, and the remarkable thing was, she said, that I was entirely self-taught. I had been determined, and it had paid off.

Now, I felt, Mother could not turn her back on me because I could no longer be her "shining star" to reflect glory and honor on her. She would be forced to love me just for myself. I could, and did, do all the things she wanted and expected of me, and I could still make her proud of me, for I would grow up to be *somebody.* It would simply be in a different field of accomplishment; if I couldn't be a concert pianist, I would explore other options and determine at what I might succeed.

Music has, of course, remained an integral part of my life, leading to other avenues of expression such as learning to play the pipe organ for church, teaching piano, even playing for various church choirs and soloists. I had never dreamed that college, for me, would not contain a music scholarship. Instead, under different and heightened circumstances, I pursued a career in medical technology, where my hearing loss was not as vital, and the skills in coping I had devel-

Announcement for Shirley's appearance on Morris B. Sachs's *Amateur Hour* program, 1946. Copyrighted material used by permission of *The Truth*.

On Amateur Hour

Shirley Gordon, 16-year-old daughter of Mr. and Mrs. William Gordon, 1010 Lafayette, a pianist, will play on the Morris B. Sachs amateur hour Sunday.

Miss Gordon is a high school senior and is pianist for the school choir. She is a former pupil of Miss Mary Elizabeth Miller and of Miss Clara Kantzler of the Academy of Music, and is now a student of Miss Charlotte Raatz.

Friends may vote for her by sending postal card to the Morris B. Sachs amateur hour, 6638 Halstead, Chicago.

oped made for quite a rewarding career. The accuracy and precision necessary to succeed in that field greatly appealed to me, and I was quite adept at it. My choice surprised a lot of people, but only because they had never known of my hearing loss or my fascination and absorption with neatness, orderliness, and reliability. I had learned those lessons well from my beloved grandmother: "A place for everything and everything in its place." That was how she had kept her household; I did the same in the laboratory.

Although my deafness loomed as a limiting factor in my life, through determination and willpower I wanted to be able to turn it into a positive and transforming experience. I vowed I would never let it hold me back from accomplishing whatever I wanted to do in my life; instead, I would make suitable substitutions and accommodations to turn my life into an enriching, positive, and even rewarding one. I wanted to succeed through trial and error, thereby learning early what I could and could not do, but never being afraid to make the effort. I somehow knew it was better to have tried and failed than never to have tried at all.

The Jam Jar

At the corner of Marion and Second streets, near a Sinclair service station, stood a building that had once been the Inter-Urban Station for the electric cars that ran from Elkhart to South Bend. It had now been turned into an after-school club for high schoolers called the Jam Jar, a place they could go for dancing (called "jamming" in those days) and playing games like shuffleboard, Chinese checkers, and backgammon, or just plain socializing. Refreshments were available, with sodas being the strongest drinks served.

A founding committee had been established to set up rules, regulations, and requirements for membership. Shortly after the Jam Jar's opening, Charles stopped in after school and surprisingly was welcomed by the other students. However, one of his former classmates told me that some parents made phone calls to the committee to protest his presence, with one father being so vulgar and vituperative in his language that his daughter, who overheard the conversation, was sickened and shocked by his coarse words: she still has those feelings even though more than sixty years have passed. She was on the founding committee, so she was in a position to know what went on.

Charles was not only accepted as a member but was elected to serve on the social committee, helping to plan the Jam Jar's activities. This was the closest he came to participating in the social life of his peers, away from school and unrelated to athletic or musical events, and he reveled in it. The grace of his wiry, athletic frame also made him a natural-born dancer, a talent he had inherited from Mother; however, the rules stipulated that white girls and colored boys simply weren't allowed to dance together.

The Jam Jar was a place where Charles could mingle, laugh, and talk, and for a while feel as though he were truly one of them. There was a jukebox with all the latest records, but often he sat down at the piano and picked out popular tunes while the other students gathered around, laughing, singing, and dancing. He had a natural ability to play almost any musical instrument he picked up, and the piano was one of them.

Years later, a former classmate told me that one evening while she was waiting for a ride home from her father, Charles showed her how to do a few dance steps, something other than the "two-step" that was all she knew how to do, right out there on the sidewalk in front of the Jam Jar. She said he had been a perfect gentleman the whole time. Perhaps she thought he would make a pass at her; most white people seem to think all colored boys can't wait to get their hands on a white girl.

Her regret was that, because of prejudices, he was not allowed to show her those steps *inside* the club; the one time he *had* danced with a white girl, both he and the girl got a severe reprimand and orders that this was never to happen again. It did, however, work both ways: just a year or two later, a male classmate danced with a colored girl at one of the open-air summer band concerts, and he was merely called "a bad boy." This male classmate told me that the girl Charles had danced with was very pretty, and so was the girl *he* had danced with, even though neither could remember the girls' names! The classmate stated quite candidly, "A pretty girl is a pretty girl."

One day there was a meeting of the social committee, and of course Charles was there, seated at a long table with the rest of the committee members. Down the sidewalk came some "rednecks," a group of white men who were up from the South and working in a local factory for the war effort. Seeing Charles as they passed by, they doubled back and rushed into the room, cursing and becoming quite abusive in their protestations that "no nigger should be sittin' next to no white girls."

Quite calm and composed, the adult supervisor—a woman employed by the city to oversee the club's activities—asked them to show their membership cards, which quite obviously they couldn't possibly have had. When they were unable to produce the cards, she advised them they would have to leave the premises, as the club was open to members only. With much swearing and verbal abuse, the men left, but not before shaking their fists and glaring pointedly at Charles, vowing to come back on Saturday night and "wreck the joint."

Charles didn't want to be the cause of any trouble, and these roughly dressed, tough-looking men seemed more than capable of making good on their threats, so he offered to quit the Jam Jar and resign his membership on the committee. The committee indignantly refused to even consider his offer. Apparently the students were more open-minded about having a person of color in their midst than were their parents or these men.

That Saturday night dance was looked forward to with some trepidation on the students' part. The group of rednecks showed up as threatened, ready to do battle, only to find the doors blocked and the building completely surrounded by a turnout of the entire student body, standing four and five deep on the sidewalks. The men couldn't gain entrance without fighting the white kids, and this they were evidently not prepared to do. Frustrated, their group finally broke up, drove off, and left the students alone.

It was undoubtedly the decisions, actions, and support of the Jam Jar board and its members that contributed to the reactions of the students and caused them to demonstrate in the way they did. After all, hadn't they welcomed Charles into all their various activities prior to this time? Hadn't he been an outstanding, exemplary student and athlete, contributing much to the school's glory? I considered this night a perfect example of the high regard his fellow students exhibited for Charles.

The year 1944 was not an auspicious time for colored people, especially those who might "look white" or "act white," not even in the North. And, perish the thought, some might even feel they were "as good as a white person." Looking as he did, Charles was

Charles (*in tan hat on the back row*) at the Jam Jar, an after-school club where high schoolers could dance ("jam" in those days); play shuffleboard, Chinese checkers, and backgammon; or socialize. Sodas were the strongest beverage served. 1943–44 high school yearbook. Used by permission of Elkhart Community Schools.

left in limbo, desperately seeking to find a world into which he fit. For him, Elkhart had in so many ways truly become no place to be somebody.

The Jam Jar unfortunately didn't last very long, only from 1943 to 1944, but it filled a definite need for students to have someplace to go that was approved by their parents. The experiences Charles garnered there were impressed upon his memory, not always favorably, for a lifetime. There was acceptance on one hand, rejection on another, and he could never predict in advance which it would be, or from which group of people.

Like many other boys in his class, he entered the armed services upon graduation, for there was a war on. Those boys fought for their friends and families as well as for the "rednecks" of the world.

Strangely enough, perhaps because he was living at our grandparents' house, I don't believe our family ever heard about the Saturday night incident at the Jam Jar until many years later, when it was related to me by Ted Strouse, a friend and former classmate. It was easy for Charles to forget that in that place, Elkhart, he *had* been considered somebody, and some good things *had* happened to him there.

Murder in a Small Town

On September 14, 1945, there was a murder in Elkhart. Homicide statistics were very low in our small town; after all, you knew almost everyone there or you knew their families. It was the kind of place where, as you walked down the street or sat in your porch swing, people would say hi, and you knew to whom you were speaking. It was the quality of your life: you knew your neighbors and friends, and in turn they knew you and your family; these were people who knew who you were, where you were coming from, and pretty much where you were going. These were not folks who solved their problems by killing each other; that sort of thing might occur in "wicked" large cities like New York, Chicago, or Los Angeles, but not in a quiet little town like Elkhart. A homicide was really a rarity, and a total shocker.

The victim, fifteen-year-old Sally Young, lived just half a block from our house. Through tall, leafy trees and front yards of green grass, I could see her home from my bedroom window. We shared the same December birth month—she on the ninth, me on the thirtieth—in the same year, 1929. We had attended Lincoln Elementary School together, played on the same swings and May poles, and engaged in vigorous games of kickball on the playground. It was on that playground she met her death.

Murder in a small town, 1945. Montage of headlines/articles from the *Elkhart Truth* newspaper. Copyrighted material used by permission of *The Truth*.

The Elkhart T
THE HOME NEW
EK SLAYI
Knifed on Schoo
und; Gasps Me
ion Before Deat
Seek to Link Negro in Knife Mur
Identified by Stabbed Man
Simple Funeral Services Held For Slain Child
THE HOME NEWSPAPER FOR ELKHART COUN
ELKHART, INDIANA, TUESDAY, OCTOBER 30, 1945.
ELKHART MAN C
MURDER OF S
Virgil Swinehart Tells Complete Story of Fatal Playground Attack
Describes Wanderings, Leading to Texas; Worried Over Deed and Wanted to Give up, Says Statement
SALLY JOAN YOUNG
Letter Carrier Finds Knife Not Far From Friday Murder Scene
Sent for Study to FBI, With Other Possible Evidence
Virgil Swinehart Is Indicted for Death of 15-Year-Old Sally Young
Grand Jury Makes Report at Close of Week-Long Inquiry
To Be Taken to Michigan City Prison Thursday
The concluding chapter in the sordid story of the knife slaying of an Elkhart High school sophomore girl in an Elkhart churchyard last autumn was written in a South Bend courtroom this morning.
Almost 7 months after 15-year-old Sally Joan Young died in General hospital after being unnaturally assaulted and stabbed, her confessed slayer, Virgil J. Swinehart, 31-year old Elkhart carnival worker, was sentenced to life imprisonment by Judge Dan Pyle. Sentencing took place shortly before 10:30 this morning in the St. Joseph county circuit court, where on Feb. 21 Swinehart had pleaded guilty.
Manner Changes

We knew her parents, her younger sisters, and her small brother. Her father ran his own business repairing cars in the garage in their backyard. Daddy said he was an excellent mechanic, and even had him do some work on our family car. We knew her folks had gone through a bitter divorce, one that ended up with her mother leaving the kids with their father. Since Sally was the oldest, she acted like a mother hen looking out for her brood; she "mothered" them, and they adored her.

On that night Sally had gone to a movie with a friend who lived just across the street. Mr. Young wasn't present that night, so when a knock on the door came shortly after her return home, it was Sally who answered. A man stood there, and police thought he may have lured her from the house by telling her he had a car he wanted her dad to fix. He explained it was parked over by the school; he would show her where it was and the next day she could have her dad bring it home and repair it. Neighbors who lived on the corner next door to the Youngs said they heard Sally laughing and talking to a man as they headed toward the school yard, apparently under no coercion.

But there, in the same place she had played as a child, he raped her, then stabbed and horribly mutilated her after she threatened to tell what he had done to her sexually; he then ran away. Sally managed to stagger across the street to a house on the corner where the Schnell family lived; a porch light was on as the parents sat waiting up for their daughters to return from a football game. Sally collapsed into a chair in their living room, begging for help as she bled profusely. Mrs. Schnell called the police, then an ambulance, and Sally was rushed to the hospital. With her dying breath, when asked if she knew who had done this dreadful thing, she said it was a colored man. Her four-year-old sister had evidently been awakened by the sounds of Sally coming in; when questioned, the child said, "A big black man came and took Sally away."

The town was in an uproar. Headlines in the *Elkhart Truth* newspaper read: "Seek Slayer of Girl, 15" (September 15, 1945); "Seek to

Link Negro in Knife Murder" (September 17, 1945); "Letter Carrier Finds Knife Not Far From Friday Murder Scene" (September 18, 1945).

The police demanded and received from Mr. Young a list of all the colored men who had ever come to his garage, and they interrogated every one of them, including Daddy. How hurt and angry our family was to think that the police *dared* question our daddy, who had been in his usual place after 9:00 p.m.: in bed, sound asleep.

Rumors ran rampant for several weeks. Only two blocks from the crime scene, a letter carrier had found a knife they thought was the murder weapon. A young Negro was arrested and held in jail because earlier in the evening, he had stabbed a man near the railroad yards in a robbery attempt. The police also rounded up about forty-five Mexican railroad track workers to question them about the murder, but were unable to tie any of these non-English-speaking men to the case.

Another result of this case was that it brought to light numerous incidents of skulkers in the months just prior to the murder, reports of men lurking in the shadows and peering in the windows of homes. How could those things have been happening and not have been brought to the public's attention?

From all these reports after the murder occurred, Leah literally became a nervous wreck, consumed by paranoia. She was afraid to sleep alone in her own room at night, tearfully begging and pleading with me to let her share the bed with me lest someone climb in the second-story window and abduct her. With all three of our brothers away in the armed services, we each now had our own bedroom, but I think she remembered only too vividly the ease with which Charles used to climb up there through the window when he had been out late.

Then, on October 30, 1945, the headlines changed: "Elkhart Man Confesses to Murder of Sally Young"; "Virgil Swinehart Is Indicted for Death of 15-Year-Old Sally Young" (November 15, 1945).

According to police, the man (a former taxi driver) was seen loitering in front of a local jewelry store window, and an alert salesman had reported the "suspicious" activity to the police. Under questioning, the man confessed to the murder and led the police to the murder weapon, a knife he had tossed on the grounds of the Swedish Lutheran Church, immediately adjacent to the playground crime area.

Virgil Swinehart was a swarthy, black-haired, beetle-browed man. On the night of the murder, he had been wearing a navy pea jacket with the collar standing up and a dark knit ski cap pulled well down over his forehead. To a child of four, only slightly awake, he could have looked like a "big black man." He underwent trial and was subsequently sentenced to life in Michigan State Prison, where if alive, he is still incarcerated. He was white—not colored, not Mexican, but *white*.

Daddy heaved a great sigh of relief: "You know, for a few weeks there I was almost afraid to go to work because white folks were looking at *me* with such suspicion and hatred, I felt they might jump me at any minute. I was really scared there for a while, because I knew I hadn't done anything, but they acted like I might have!"

Waves of indignation ran through the town, particularly among the colored population. Tensions at one point ran so high and were so racially intense that most colored people felt there was great danger of a lynching of the young man initially arrested for the robbery attempt. The white people in town were afraid too of possible race riots. It was then that the *Elkhart Truth* printed an editorial, placing it on the front page for all to see, in which they stated the community owed the colored and Mexican populations a deep apology for the way suspicions had descended upon them and for the shabby manner in which they had been treated, all because of their color and/or ethnic background.

I was going to graduate from high school in June 1947, a mere two years away. I could hardly wait to shake the dust off my feet and leave that prejudiced small town behind; I had truly had enough, particularly in view of the exemplary conduct our parents had always presented in public. I was in full agreement with Charles's later statement that Elkhart truly was "no place to be somebody."

Graduation Ceremonies for Dark Young People

So wholeheartedly and energetically had Charles participated in club, musical, and athletic events that he was widely known and highly esteemed by both his teachers and his fellow students, as well as by the many adults throughout the city who had enjoyed his performances and accomplishments. It was quite evident that he was not a shy, retiring individual, but one who gloried in being a leader.

The same reasoning occurred in my young mind; still, it wasn't something we consciously thought about. It was simply recognition from others that we were the best at whatever we tried to do. What Mother couldn't force, however, was acceptance of us on a personal level, a level that went deeper than outward show—an exchange back and forth of our innermost feelings, a recognition of our reality as human beings.

It wasn't until our senior high school years that we first began to realize what a dream world we had been living in, and at that time we began to fathom that certain things would never change. We would never be completely accepted by those white people because of our skin color—not by those people in that bastion of narrow-mindedness that screamed, "So far, and no further!"

How naive we were to think that since we had been allowed such total involvement and interaction with the other students and white adults, it meant anything other than an enjoyment on their part of pulling the strings that made those two colored kids perform. It was the same principle as that of white men in the South getting little black children to dance a jig for them; it was a demonstration of power. But if it crossed our minds at all, we both believed we had transcended the racial barrier and that for us such a thing didn't exist.

Most of Elkhart's other colored people felt the same way toward our family: we had acted like, thought like, and associated so much with white people that they looked on us as being more white than colored. What we were, and where we were, was in limbo, belonging neither to one side nor the other.

Few people ever knew Charles's feelings of hurt, rejection, and despair when he was unable to get a date with any of the girls in his class for the senior prom. Even if she had wanted to, no white girl would have been permitted to attend with him; both her parents and the school board would have forbidden it. And of course it was Mother who, with her usual resourcefulness, made the school board an offer they could not refuse: give Charles special permission to bring a colored girl from out of town to be his date for this occasion. I think the board heaved a collective sigh of relief when they accepted this "perfect solution."

Marian Finlay was a fair-skinned and shapely girl, with beautiful hair and a modest demeanor; she was the daughter of family friends from Michigan. The invitation was merely another of Mother's ploys to get her way with the white "powers that be," for there was no romance or matchmaking involved. This was the way she had fought for us from our childhood days. She was determined that Charles was going to be allowed to take part in *all* of his graduation activities, without being excluded from any merely because of his color.

Charles told the rest of the family he felt he'd had the last and best laugh, for when he met Marian at the train station she turned out to be far more attractive than any of the white girls who had refused to go to the prom with him because of his color; in fact, she was fairer complexioned than they were and could easily have "passed"

Charles Gordon, 1944 graduation photo. Activities credited in the yearbooks during his high school years of 1941–44: HI-Y, Dramatics Club, Yell Club, Annual Ad Staff, Student Council, Choir (Pres.), Cross Country (Capt.), Track (Capt.), Boys' Glee Club, Tumbling Team, Blue Jackets, Superintendent's Council. Used by permission of Elkhart Community Schools.

for white. Although the rest of us didn't dance (religion, again!), Charles did, and he was as graceful and impressive on the dance floor as he had ever been on the athletic field. He and Marian, pardon the pun, "had a ball."

One Sunday afternoon shortly before baccalaureate and commencement exercises, I was in the living room practicing on the piano when I heard what seemed to be the sound of crying coming from the kitchen. I snuck quietly to the kitchen door, where I saw Charles with his arms around Mother, who was weeping as if her heart would break. "What's the matter?" I queried.

Charles turned to me, with an angry expression on his face I had never seen before, and said, "You get back in there and practice and mind your own business!" I fled.

Later, after Charles had left, I asked Mother what had happened. She told me that Charles didn't want her and Daddy to attend his graduation exercises because they were "colored," and he would be embarrassed to introduce them as his parents. I was speechless. How could he be ashamed of his own parents, particularly for that reason, since everyone in town had always known he was colored too?

Mulling over the reason Mother had given me, it simply didn't ring true. I felt somehow there had to be deeper issues, for what she had said made no sense. I thought of his "declaration of independence" in his junior year, when he moved to our grandparents' home despite Mother's angry protests. She hadn't wanted him to be independent of her, desiring instead that everything he did reflect glory upon *her* as his mother.

I now saw this in a new light; Charles was trying to separate and remove himself from Mother's dominance—a "weaning process," if you will. He wanted to strike out on his own, knowing full well he could never do this if he remained at 1010 Lafayette Street under Mother's control. The strictness of her religion, her stringent rules and regulations that banned all the things he wanted to try, made

Shirley Gordon, photograph taken shortly after 1947 high school graduation. Activities credited in 1947 yearbook: *Pennant* weekly school newspaper (feature writer), Paint and Palette Art Club, A Capella Choir (pianist).

whatever successes he already had achieved even sweeter, for he had done them on his own terms.

My musings caused me to believe his reluctance to have Mother and Daddy attend his graduation exercises stemmed from Charles's deep-rooted feelings that they were only interested in hearing people exclaim about how proud they must be. He felt he had come this far alone, under trying circumstances, and would not willingly share the credit with them.

Sad to say, it is true they would have tried to give people the impression that *they* were the reason he had accomplished so much. In all good conscience, he felt he was responsible for his own successes and therefore deserved the credit. His own pride necessitated reaching for the stars and letting nothing stand in his way. This was not something I could ever discuss with Mother, however, for it would have implied criticism of her actions, which she most definitely would not tolerate.

I also wondered, after that, if his seeming acceptance on so many levels by Elkhart's white people had made him feel that he was, in the final analysis, a white person. Or had he worn that white mask for so long and in so many ways that he believed denying the reality of his blackness would *make* him white? We all knew that away from musical and sports events he had been compelled to live in a black world. Was this the result of our total belief in our parents' oft-repeated dictum: "Color doesn't matter, it's what you are *inside* that counts?" Fine, if you are white; it's an entirely different matter if you are colored.

I didn't understand the schisms that had been created by our upbringing, nor did I understand Charles's confused inner feelings until several years later when it was my turn to graduate. Had I known even some of Charles's experiences, I could have saved myself a lot of grief.

One young redheaded boy, Ernie, whom for several years I had accompanied on the piano at area vocal contests, had taken me to the senior class play in the late autumn. I had been given permission to attend with him because Mother knew his mother, and although his family was white, they had always been very nice to us. Someone must have given Ernie some static about his taking a colored girl to that play, but I didn't know about that until it was almost time for the first event of the 1947 graduating class. This was a traditional processional on Senior Class Day, in which the entire senior class walked by twos across the auditorium stage. Time was nearing for this event, and I hadn't been asked by any boy in my class to march with him. It was a considerable loss of face to have to march with another girl, but since there were more girls than boys, it was inevitable that some girls would have to march together. Seeing Ernie in the hall one day after school, I asked him to be my partner for Senior Class Day.

He blushed, a red so vivid that his face matched his hair, as he vehemently protested, "Oh, no, I can't do that!"

Puzzled, I asked him, "Why not?"

Quite forcefully, he replied, "What would people think and what would they say if they saw me walking across the stage with a *colored* girl?"

Taken aback, I could only walk away, but through my mind ran pictures of the number of times and hours over the years the two of us had rehearsed after school for those vocal contests, alone in the practice room, without the subject of our racial differences ever coming up. I wasn't asking him to be my sweetheart, just my friend.

Evidently I still wasn't getting the picture, for in my naivete I went to the teacher who was one of our class sponsors, explained to her that I didn't want to march with a girl, and asked for her help in finding a boy I could walk with. Now, my Aunt Bea had worked as a housekeeper for this very same teacher years before, so I felt that since the teacher knew our family, she would be able to come up with a male partner for me. She did say she would see what she could do, but nothing came of it. In saddened retrospect, I asked myself,

"How could you be so *dumb?* Of course she, a white teacher, wasn't about to force a white boy to march with you!"

Senior Class Day arrived. To my utter dismay, not only did I have to walk with a girl, but an obese one at that. With no other choice, I stumbled along on the inside, she on the outside, while I tried to hide myself behind her obesity. The difficult part was, she was a girl whom I did know and very much liked, but not as a partner on this special day!

Even after the chagrin of having a female partner, I proceeded to participate in the class program that immediately followed. I played piano with the senior class band, accompanied several soloists, and performed a piano solo myself—but when the day was ended, I went home and wept copiously over the blow to my ego.

The only colored boy in my class had previously asked me to walk with him and I had turned him down, thinking that surely one of my white friends—with whom I thought I had much more in common—would come forward to walk with me. So, I had definitely been hoisted on my own petard, as Hamlet would have said, because when I asked him as a last resort to march with me, he just laughed and said he had already asked another colored girl to be his partner.

All my previous experiences with people's efforts to deny me equal opportunities had still not sunk in. Always in some shape, form, or fashion, there had been deliverance of some sort, a method of salvation; help had always materialized—through Mother, a teacher, or *someone.* But from graduation day forward, and upon my entrance to college, I knew I had to come to grips myself, with *myself.* There would be nothing to cushion me from the reality that the world considered me as a colored girl, regardless of my talents, my accomplishments, or my appearance. Therefore, I would have to show them that I was content and happy with who I was and that I firmly believed in myself, and let the onus of prejudice be on *them.* From that day forward, Elkhart would not be my world.

It wasn't until some time later that Charles and I each discovered the message we wanted to proclaim to the world. It was not a message of concern over the color of our skin: that had, by now, simply become unimportant and irrelevant. It was the realization that the most important belief of all was in our own humanity and the humanity of all the world's peoples. It was the knowledge that we too—first, foremost, and above all—were *human beings.*

We could now know with no denial, but with true realization, that underneath our skin we were exactly the same as everyone else; we had found our own reality. That knowledge ringed our minds in a light that eventually would shine forth to all with whom we came in contact. We had recognized our own humanity, our membership in the human race, and would not ever again let anyone take that away from us. To deny anyone that recognition is to shrivel their souls, and we both, Charles and me, had an incredible determination not to let that be our fate!

Photograph by Wayne Crosslin of Charles Gordone; © 1977 and used by permission of the *St. Louis Post-Dispatch*.

Epilogue

The Pathway Leading to a New Life in the West

LAYERS

Layer upon layer of pain,
Of loss of identity . . .
Layers wrapping, hiding,
Overlapping, building, hardening . . .
Layers of neglect,
Feelings of no love,
Of no recognition of individuality . . .
Layers of insecurity,
Layers without love,
Layers of fear of abandonment,
Of being set adrift . . .
Layers of fear of loss of
Closeness to Mother Earth,
To nature . . .
Layers that prevent one from

Hearing the silence, the quiet,
To be at ease in being alone . . .
Layers that won't allow you
To be the Man, the Father,
Because Father-Figure was
Emasculated, torn down . . .
Layers revealing feet of clay
And exposed with gnashing of teeth
And rending of garments . . .
Layers calcified
Into mummy-like wrappings,
Making you unable to see,
To hear, to taste, to smell, to touch . . .
Until one came and gently,
Oh, so gently,
Began to soak, to soften,
To strip away layer after layer
All the dead wrappings
From your soul . . .
Then came your resurrection,
Your soul's rebirth . . .
And when your vision saw with
New eyes, a new life, a new worthiness,
This new encapsulation of love,
Of unconditional love,
Your epiphany came not in recognition
Of a past life with its discarded layers,
But of your new self.

Shirley Gordon Jackson

From the heart to the mind and back again, the story of Charles, our mother, and me continues to cross back and forth, weaving our souls and lives together like a multi-patterned piece of fabric that may have a hole here or a tear there, yet remains indestructible enough to forever shape the textures and designs of our lives.

From the very beginning our mother believed in prenatal influences, and so, while pregnant with her firstborn, Charles Edward, she spent hours every day at a Catholic cathedral in Cleveland, Ohio, totally immersed in the beautiful music that poured from the mighty pipe organ. She often cited this exposure as the primary reason for Charles's outstanding musical ability. Indeed, this love for music and the ability to perform it was also inherited by her other children. With Stanley on the violin, Leah on the cello, me at the piano, and Mother singing soprano along with Charles's glorious tenor voice, while Cecil formed a vociferous cheering section, we had our very own small "Sound of Music" family.

It was the uplifting words of James Weldon Johnson's "Lift Ev'ry Voice and Sing" that was initially impressed on our thinking, especially Charles's, for on all those occasions when we performed at local colored churches—and they were numerous—this song was always on the program. In a few short years it became widely known as the "Negro National Anthem." While Charles believed intensely in the song's message, he stoutly maintained that "The Star-Spangled Banner" was *his* national anthem; even at this early age he was beginning to see a vision of an America that was shared by all peoples.

Charles's childhood years have never before been chronicled, for the simple reason that no one else possesses this information. As the sole surviving family member, only I am left to relate those childhood memories, all of which remain forever etched upon my heart and mind.

Stanley was the quiet, shy, and retiring middle brother, and the very epitome of the phrase "tall, dark, and handsome." If, as Grandmother often said, he was the one of the boys who looked exactly like his father, Charles Fleming must certainly have been a handsome fellow! Seemingly with no effort on Stanley's part, all the ladies loved him, which used to yank my brother Charles's chain no end.

After Stanley's stint of service in the Merchant Marine, he stayed in Elkhart for a few months before joining our Uncle Al in Berkeley, California. Soon married, he settled in Oakland, California, working at an aluminum manufacturing plant for the remainder of his working days. He and his wife were members of the Masons organization and led quite an active social life therein.

Stanley had three children—one daughter and two sons, all of whom reside in central California. He passed away in the mid-1980s, leaving me with fond memories of our younger days when, as children, we played our various instruments as a musical trio. In later life, he played the violin only for his own personal enjoyment.

Cecil, the third son, was the more gregarious and outgoing—sometimes brash—personality. Those in Elkhart who remember him speak fondly and humorously of him as the class cut-up. During a portion of Charles's years in New York City, Cecil lived with him there, but after just a few years he moved back to Elkhart, then to Chicago, and then to Niles, Michigan, where he served at one time as sheriff. He was a very restless person, seemingly unable to find and pursue his true path in life. Cecil died just a month before our mother and is the only one of the five siblings buried in the family plot in Grace Lawn Cemetery in Elkhart.

Leah married and lived at my grandparents' house for a few months before she and her husband took off for California. We never grew close, even though I saw her occasionally, for her lifestyle was entirely different than mine. (To this very day I don't like or want to be around alcoholics!) She divorced her husband shortly after their arrival in California, although she did remarry several years later. Like Ora, she never seemed to make good choices as to a life companion. And her hatred of both Mother and Daddy made it uncomfortable for me to be around her for very long.

Leah never had children, and I think it was one of the deepest regrets of her life. It seemed such a waste for her to die at the relatively young age of fifty-six.

Following his graduation from high school, Charles entered the U.S. Army Air Force and was stationed in the Aleutians. It was quite evident he experienced severe trauma in those Islands, for he would never speak about his tour of duty there. For the first time in his life he lived in completely segregated conditions, which was totally alien to anything he had known before. Everything in the service was highly regimented, however, which he said made him feel right at home because his younger years had been so intensely structured by our mother.

Upon his discharge Charles returned briefly to Indiana, where he soon married Juanita Barton of South Bend, Indiana. The marriage was approved by Mother, albeit half-heartedly, because the bride belonged to Mother's religious denomination and a baby was already on the way, Mother's first grandchild. Charles and Juanita had two children: a son, Stephen, and a daughter, Judy. They separated in 1951 but did not divorce until 1992.

In California, Charles enrolled in the drama department at L.A. City College, where he studied from 1948 to 1952 and earned his B.A. (He would later, in 1957, attend New York and Columbia Universities and obtain his M.A.) He was one of just two colored students in the class, and it quickly became apparent that few roles were available to him. He wanted to play the roles created by Shakespeare, Ibsen, and Strindberg, but found himself cast only in subservient roles: the butler or servant who announced, "Dinner is served."

Charles wrote a scathing letter to the school newspaper; it stirred up a hornet's nest in the drama department and resulted in a change in the department's casting policy. But after college, finding that Hollywood and the film industry had little to offer him, he decided to head for New York, even though he had been cautioned by one of his professors that the situation there was just as bleak. And so, this visionary and ambitious young man of such extraordinary talent moved to New York City in 1952.

Soon after his arrival in New York, Charles joined Actors Equity and discovered another young actor named Charles Gordon was already a member. To avoid possible confusion, he decided to change *his* name by taking the "E" of his middle initial and adding it to his last name, thereby becoming "Gordone." (The accented second syllable rhymes with "lone.") Inherently a professional decision—although it also appealed to his flair for the dramatic—it didn't affect any of the remaining Gordons, which accounts for the continued spelling of my name.

Despite landing a role on Broadway within a few months, he found there were infrequent acting and directing jobs for artists of any color other than white. It was during this period that Gordone helped found the Committee for the Employment of Negro Performers. It had some measure of success, but he was still not fulfilling his youthful vision and ambition.

In 1959 Gordone began a relationship with Jeanne Warner; they had a daughter in 1963, and in 1965 he had a son with another woman. In 1973 his relationship with Ms. Warner ended.

When he wrote *No Place to Be Somebody*, won the Pulitzer in 1970, and began to publicly express his youthful vision of a shared America, it put him in direct opposition to the Black Nationalists rising at that time. Furthermore, he said to me, the demands of celebrity, the conflicts of racial politics, and the unprotected selling of the play's film rights in perpetuity—in addition to thousands of dollars' worth of producer's debts left to him—drove him into a kind of exile. It all exacted a toll on both his life and his career from which it would take over two decades to recover.

In 1978, Gordone returned to his native Midwest, this time to Park College in St. Louis, Missouri, where he had been invited to direct and teach, still holding fast to his deeply formed and lifelong dream of a shared America.

It was in 1981 that he first met Susan Kouyomjian while directing a play in San Francisco, and he discovered that she shared his vision. A year later, she founded the American Stage in Berkeley, California—the first multiracial theater in the San Francisco Bay area—and invited him to join her. Thus, they were able to embark on their mutual vision of dramatizing a shared America. It was this association that led, before much time had passed, to their marriage. Gordone asked her to be his life partner and help him start anew. My brother told me in a tender voice that one of his later life's greatest joys was the happiness and sense of fulfillment he felt when he united with Susan Kouyomjian in 1987. Gordone and Susan remained married until the time of his death in 1995.

During his long period of recovery, he contacted Juanita Barton with the hope of making amends. She, in turn, confessed that although she had remarried, she had never finalized a divorce from Gordone, despite telling others she had. Juanita, now a widow, and Charles agreed to finalize their divorce, which was done in Brazos County, Texas, in 1992. Juanita died a year later.

Continuing his efforts to rectify some of his past errors, Gordone also renewed contact with his children. With almost his last remaining asset, he turned over title and ownership of eighteen to twenty acres of land in Woodstock, New York, with a trailer home on them, to his daughter, Leah Carla. He also spent much time in Elkhart in order to help our parents, now quite a bit older, in their time of need.

It was Susan who actually mapped out the plans for their new lives. Gordone had begun another play, one with a Western setting, and she pointed out to him that for the sake of authenticity, they must move west and be steeped in Western lore in order for the play to ring true. It was she who read of Texas A&M University's need for an instructor in their Speech Communications and Theatre Arts department. She was the partner who saw the unlimited possibilities and helped secure him a D. H. Lawrence Fellowship in San

Cristobal, New Mexico, as well as a position as the visiting scholar in residence at the Amerind Foundation in Dragoon, Arizona.

Assisting him in this new phase of their life together, Susan did much of the work in seeking out and bringing numerous multiracial Westerners to his classroom to share their stories of the old ways with him and his students, in a series titled American Voices. She also arranged for him to be the guest speaker or moderator at many Western symposia. It was no wonder, then, that Gordone told her that it was *her* work that had made his life meaningful.

Charles Gordone had labored mightily and been rewarded with a multifaceted career. He had been an actor, director, playwright, educator, and activist. A list of his career achievements attests to the extensive dimensions of his talent. He was a guest artist and instructor at Park College (Missouri); the Cell Block Theatre Program, New Jersey State Prison System; the New School of Social Research, New York; Sarah Lawrence University; and Hendrix College, Conway, Arkansas. He was the Director-in-Residence of the American Stage Theater in Berkeley, California; a Distinguished Lecturer in the Department of Speech, Communication, and Theatre Arts at Texas A&M University, Bryan–College Station, Texas; and a Visiting Scholar at the Amerind Foundation in Dragoon, Arizona. He was an educator in every sense of the word.

A member of the Ensemble Studio Theatre, Gordone also served as chair of the Committee for the Employment of Negro Performers, served on the Presidential Commission on Civil Disorders, and was a panelist of the Texas Commission on the Arts. In addition, he was associate producer of *Nothing But A Man,* starring Abbey Lincoln, Ivan Dixon, and Julius Harris (Young & Roemer); and associate producer of *Black Like Me* (credited as Jules Tannenbaum), United Artists. He was a lifetime member of the Actors Studio.

As if the foregoing weren't enough to merit most people's attention, he also received numerous awards and honors: the Obie Award in 1953; the Critics' Circle Award, New York and Los Angeles, in

1970 and 1971; the Drama Desk Award, 1970; the Pulitzer Prize for Drama, 1970; the Vernon Rice Award, 1970; the NAACP Image Award, 1971; a National Endowment for the Arts Fellowship, 1979; the D. H. Lawrence Fellowship in Creative Writing, San Cristobal, New Mexico, 1987; the NAACP Playwright's Contribution Award, Hollywood, 1987; Visiting Scholar, Amerind Foundation, 1988 and 1992. He was honored by the American Academy of Arts and Letters in 1971 and the National Institute of Arts and Letters in 1971.

He wrote more than a dozen plays, screenplays, adaptations, and articles and directed more than thirty-four stage productions. He directed, acted, and had his work produced on Broadway, off-Broadway, at Carnegie Hall, in Europe, and in American regional, college, and community theaters, while his acting credits include roles in professional theater, television, and film.

Yet even after all that, he said one of the most thrilling experiences of his life occurred when Susan arranged a trip to Goliad, Texas, to visit some of the African American cowboys of mixed ancestry still living there. They told Gordone of their lengthy history working on the ranches, and he learned from them of the legendary cowboy Bill Pickett, who invented the art of bulldogging now seen in all Western rodeos.

What a joy, inspiration, and satisfaction it would have been for him to have known about these men as a teenager, when he affected the Western dress of cowboys but was ridiculed by white and colored alike: "There's no such thing as a colored cowboy." Charles stood his ground, as he related in his last public speech (at the Autry Western Heritage Museum in Los Angeles in June 1995), stoutly averring, "Well, there is *now!*" This was just another example of history books' omissions relating to the contributions of people of color in America's development. Meeting those cowboys gave him a sense of pride in his African American heritage he had never thought he would experience in a meaningful context during his life in the West.

Although Gordone has been gone since 1995, stricken with carcinoma cholangia, a rare genetic cancer of the bile duct, he has not been forgotten by his Western friends. A number of books have been dedicated to him, and his spirit still walks in tandem with his friends. Henry Real Bird—Crow Indian poet, cowboy, writer, and artist—recognizing their shared Native American heritage and acknowledging the kindred spirits that united them, built a sweat lodge with the men of his family and invited Gordone to come and participate in that most sacred Indian ceremony, an incredible act of love and brotherhood. Frankie McWhorter, cowboy and musician, dedicated his CD *The Ranch Dance Fiddle* to Gordone's memory. A song called "Dust in the Wind" by Ramblin' Jack Elliott, recorded on one of Ramblin' Jack's latest releases, *The Long Ride,* was written in memory of Gordone, and he is still remembered at the Elko Poetry Gatherings.

There are various search engines containing over 38,000 websites on Gordone! Not all of the information on those websites is accurate, so one must be both selective and somewhat knowledgeable about Gordone. He has also been the subject of innumerable national newspaper and magazine articles, as well as countless interviews in various media.

Dr. Jerome Loving, a fellow professor at Texas A&M, published a biography in 1999 of Walt Whitman titled *Walt Whitman: The Song of Himself,* and dedicated it in part to the memory of Gordone. In the book's preface, Dr. Loving wrote:

> "One special person to thank is the late Charles Gordone, author of the play *No Place to Be Somebody,* in whose memory this book is partly dedicated. He occupied the office next to mine during most of the research and writing of this book, and I shared with him many of my discoveries and tried out many passages on him. It was the closest thing to having Whitman himself at my side as I read and wrote."[2]

Dr. Loving must have known or sensed that Gordone derived lifelong inspiration from Whitman's works; Gordone deemed him a prophet and visionary of all that was good about America. Whitman's words—particularly "I Hear America Singing," set to music and sung by the young Gordone in the high school choir—had become credos that inspired and sustained him throughout his life, a belief that there was an America worth discovering. It had to exist *somewhere!*

Not many people either could or would have followed a lifelong desire to move west. What an act of courage it must have taken to leave New York City, where he had definitely made his mark, to pursue those dreams in the last decade of his life. Paradoxically, in Texas Gordone did discover the land and peoples of his dreams. He had finally found his own place to be someone.

At the 1990 Cowboy Poetry Gathering in Elko, Nevada, Susan and Gordone heard Buck Ramsey recite his epic poem "Anthem," and a conflagration flamed in their hearts in immediate recognition of all the words Gordone had believed in for a lifetime:

". . . And as I ride out on the morning,
Before the bird, before the dawn,
I'll be this poem, I'll be this song.
Those horsemen will ride all with me,
And we'll be good and we'll be free."[3]

Later, Buck Ramsey, former Texan cowboy turned musician/writer/poet (now deceased), would write eloquently, graphically portraying and defining the cowboy funeral given Gordone in honor of his love for them and theirs for him. It was Susan who requested this ritual, making it the first time it had been enacted in a hundred years. It has now been reincarnated into the Western cowboy lore, making Gordone a legend among these people. He has given something back to them and the Western way of life he had come to love so much.

In a book published in October 1996, Ramsey wrote of this ritual in his essay for the National Endowment of the Arts Report on Traditional Folk Arts of the United States, which was distributed to Congress and libraries across the country. In 1997, the Elko Gathering reprinted 10,000 copies of this essay in their program. The cowboys, the Native Americans, and Gordone's Texas A&M students have all remained true to Gordone's vision and message of an authentic and shared America.

For Gordone, pursuing a new life in the West was not just a physical move or pat phrase: it mandated an entirely new way of thinking. His tremendous pride, fierce arrogance, and intense spirit of competition, all of which he had been force-fed along with his mother's milk and then experienced throughout his childhood in that small northern town, were further exacerbated by the treatment he received at the hands of the world. Gordone finally understood the crippling effects of the pride that had tortured him for so long. It was pride and its companion competitive spirit that had prevented him from attaining so many goals, in both his personal and professional life.

When Gordone reassessed his own values, he gained a peace that manifested itself both inwardly and outwardly. That tender loving spirit of innocence he had possessed as a child was restored to him. This was the true meaning of his new life in the West. It was in Texas that Gordone learned to love again and found himself able to follow a new pathway, one that led to his heart and resided not only in him but in the hearts of those who loved him.

Meanwhile, I found my life in California a complete turnaround from my childhood days in Indiana—and my college life and married years spent in Chicago—although I never attained the heights of eminence reached by Gordone. Life in Chicago seemed so cramped: apartments, traffic, buildings, people; everywhere one looked there was something of manmade manufacture.

I realize that living on Chicago's South Side was largely responsible for this feeling of being hemmed in. I didn't feel that way out in such suburbs as Evanston, Lake Forest, or Park Ridge; homes were spacious, surrounded by luxurious plantings of greenery. But residing in such places was a financial impossibility; in addition, they were strictly segregated at that time. There was little to appeal to my love of nature, inculcated in me from childhood by the tree-shaded streets of my hometown and nurtured by my grandmother's Native American love of all growing things.

It seemed that in Chicago, there was simply concrete everywhere—and even concrete people. To be among trees and flowers I had to go to Washington Park or Lincoln Park. While the latter also had a zoo, these were just short visits, not a place where one could reside. And winter weather in the "Windy City" seemed to last forever!

Even though I worked, like many others I rode the El train, so there was no radio to listen to. This meant the only real music I enjoyed was at church, only one day out of the week. While my husband and I did eventually buy a piano, it was difficult to find time to play on it without disturbing our neighbors in adjoining apartments. My only sources of enjoyment, after caring for my young daughter, were in reading and in my endeavors to learn the art of oil painting. After I bathed her and put her to bed for the night, my evenings were spent totally absorbed in one or the other.

The ultimate reason for my flight from Chicago, however, was that my husband, a minister who after a few years became a police officer, had become increasingly both verbally and physically abusive, not only to me, but also to our daughter. For myself, I felt if things got too aggressive I could always call the police, but what could my five-year-old daughter do? And so, we left Chicago, never looking back.

I had thought of moving to New York to join Charles and Cecil, who were both living there at the time. But it was more attractive to go someplace where the weather was much more agreeable and there were plants, flowers, and caring people everywhere. Aunt Bea and

Aunt Lula urged me to come live in California, and that is where our road west led us.

With an almost Michener-esque appreciation of the beauty of flora and fauna California displayed at every turn, I became vitally interested in horticulture, which I recognized as part of an incredible inheritance from my maternal grandmother's Native American genes. I had not known my heart would respond instantly to beauty of so many different kinds. I felt an overpowering need to express these emotions in my oil paintings, some of which now hang in private collections and in Europe. But most of all, it was the diversity of California's people and learning about their various cultures that made my heart sing a new song. It was this recognition of a greater and more satisfying life that bonded Charles and I even more closely during his Texas years.

I became a member of a lovely church in Pasadena and played the pipe organ for services in addition to my beloved piano, becoming quite in demand as an accompanist for vocal and instrumental soloists. This return to my musical roots completed my life in a way I never had dreamed possible.

After much reflection, I realize one of the few and major enjoyments of childhood, the one thing that had made life bearable for both Gordone and me, was our deep and intense involvement in music. We spent countless hours playing all the classics and old favorites, even hymns and opera, whatever seemed to flow from the deepest core of our being. As children and as adults, music had the ability to soothe, inspire, invigorate, or calm us, particularly in times of stress. I don't believe either of us had ever before realized the depths that music stirred in us. Just as books had been a magic carpet for my mind, music created a veritable tapestry of beauty that wound around my heart.

In times of crisis I have found solace in music, as did Gordone in his Western years, when his love for the art was restored to him in all of its glory. He had not performed musically in public or private in years, after his experience in high school with the adults who hadn't wanted a colored boy to sing in the white choir or perform duets with a white girl. But in his new life in the West, he had begun to sing again.

When we were children, then, Elkhart was exactly the right place to be, for the entire town was vitally interested in the total music experience, whether as listeners or as performers. We grew up knowing that Elkhart was the band-instrument manufacturing capital of the world, from C. G. Conn to Leedy, Ludwig, Buescher, Martin, and above all, the H. Selmer Company, which had only two manufacturing locations worldwide: Paris, France, and Elkhart, Indiana. Selmer was considered the Rolls-Royce of brass and reed instruments, selected by accomplished and noted musicians the world over.

In Elkhart's public school system, many of those same instruments could be rented by any student who desired to learn how to play them. Most homes owned at least a piano, and private or group lessons could be arranged, with the townspeople supportive of the recitals, concerts, and programs that were presented. If you had any musical ability or talent at all, you were with the "in crowd," but the greatest impact, always, was at your own gut level.

Leah and Stanley had been gone since the late 1980s; then in October 1993, our brother Cecil died, just a month before Mother left us. In 1995 Aunt Bea died in Texas. Two months later, in November 1995, my beloved brother Charles passed away, a mere week after Daddy's demise, leaving me the sole surviving member of a family that truly had made an impact on so many lives. The only way I could even begin to heal was to spend hours at the piano, simply playing the music we had both loved. I could still hear his voice in every note.

This book would not be complete without a depiction of my return, after an absence of many years, to the place of my birth. A high school class reunion offered me the perfect opportunity to view changes in Elkhart, both in the people and in the city itself. What a trip down memory lane!

A drive past our childhood home at 1010 Lafayette Street showed it was one of the very few houses still remaining, vacant while major repairs are going on, and looking so much smaller than I remember. The nearby vacant lots, where the neighborhood boys had played their innumerable games of baseball and softball, exist no more: factories now occupy those sites. The Calvert Coal Company? The Isbell Lumber Company? Both gone. Even the Tenth Street railroad crossing has been closed. Davidson's, the tiny one-room neighborhood grocery store at the corner of Lafayette and Oakland Avenue? Gone. My grandparents' home for over fifty years at 423 Chapman Avenue? Razed to make way for public housing. Downtown, laced with new over- and underpasses and one-way streets, was an unfamiliar maze in which I quickly became lost. Most of the major downtown stores have either closed or relocated to various malls, while the Main Street I remembered was only a dark shadow of its former self, with a lot of new buildings, and totally unfamiliar to me now.

What a lovely new river walk on North Main Street, with grassy expanses, winding paths, and curving borders outlining the Elkhart River! Island Park, where the island shaped like an elk's heart marks the divergence of the St. Joseph and Elkhart Rivers and led to the town's name, now has a new footbridge. The old silver water tower, with its large black letters spelling out "Elkhart," still stands on the south side of town. I once could see it from my grandparents' front porch. Rice Field, the scene of so many athletic triumphs for the young Gordone, has been built upon and greatly enlarged. Lincoln Elementary School up on Harrison Street, which all five of us attended, has been turned into offices for the Welfare and Social Services departments. The Carnegie Library exists no more; there's a new one in town. The YWCA where Daddy had labored so hard and long had moved years before to different and enlarged quarters. And with an explosive population growth, Elkhart now has *two* high schools. The railroads still play a vital and major role in

Charles Edward at six months, April 1926.

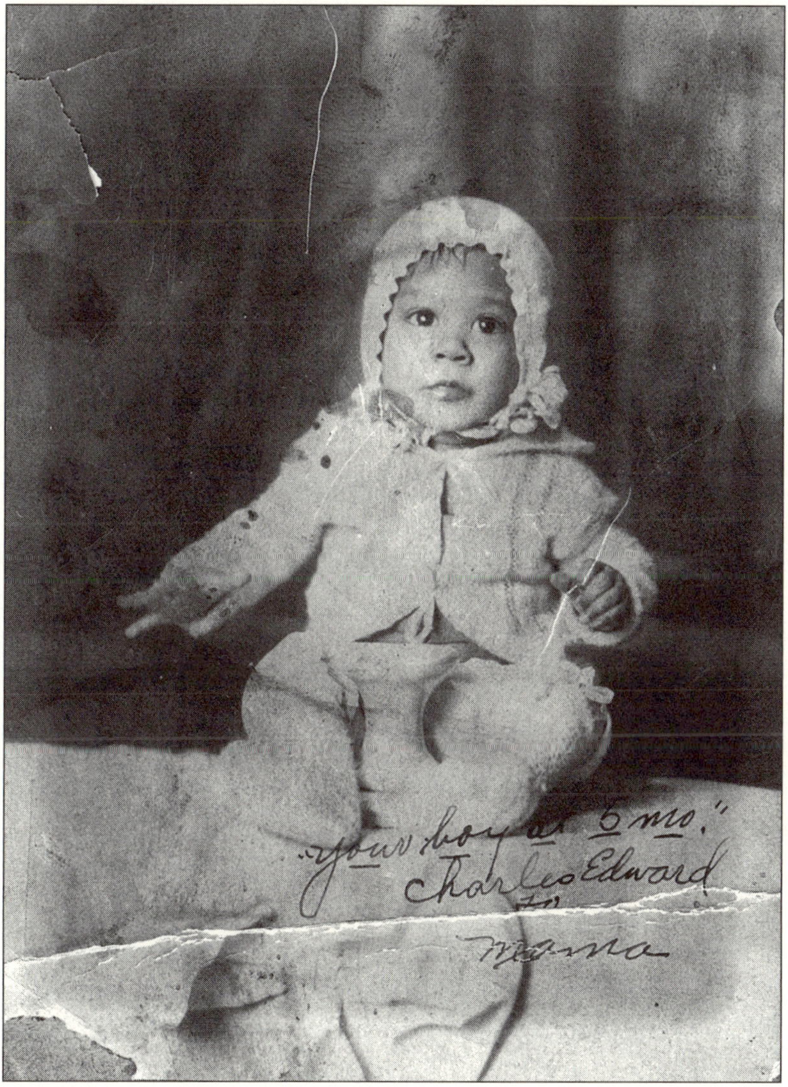

Elkhart's commerce, for major and modern switching yards have been built there, but the old train depot is still in place.

To my great delight and surprise, a meeting with the director/curator of the Elkhart County Historical Museum and his assistant, with the plus of Dr. Ervin Beck from nearby Goshen College who lectures on Gordone in addition to serving as chair for the Museum's Committee on Historic Markers, added unexpected highlights to my visit. Plans are now being made to establish a permanent exhibit honoring Gordone's many achievements, and the professor has submitted an application for a historical marker to be installed in Elkhart in Gordone's honor! Ms. Jodee Shaw, communications assistant for Elkhart Community Schools, wrote an online newsletter about Gordone and his life that went out to some three thousand people. I was nearly overwhelmed by emotion. The hope is, it will not be too long before the entire city and state recognize native son Charles Gordone and his tremendous talents and accomplishments. I know he is looking down on all this activity with that lopsided grin of his, saying, "Well done, my 'go-to' girls!"

Before bringing this book to a close, I would like to relate a few major events that occurred after Gordone died. My primary focus and basic reason for writing this book was that I wanted to share, as accurately as possible, some of our childhood experiences for posterity, as indicators of how they influenced both Gordone's life and his writings.

In addition to working on her own book, *American Seer,* Susan prepared a memorial tribute to Gordone that was presented on October 12, 2004, the anniversary of Gordone's birthday, in the J. Wayne Stark Gallery at Texas A&M, an institution that had been segregated for one hundred years. This event received front-page news coverage throughout the entire state of Texas. This tribute was also placed as an opening exhibit for the first six months of the new Brazos Valley African American Museum in Bryan–College Station, where once again press and media coverage has been extensive. Sculpture by

John Walker, paintings by Robert Schiffhauer, and many of Gordone's writings and photographs were displayed at both exhibits.

Most important, Gordone's vision of a shared and integrated America is beginning to be realized, in a manner described and predicted by Buck Ramsey as "a light that would spread from the West to the East." Like a torch, it has begun to ignite the vision of many others. The world is just now beginning to realize the truths in his vision of "inclusion" toward a shared America.

This, then, is Gordone's dream. This is his vision. This is his legacy.

I hope that throughout this book the love does shine forth, for it is indeed a love story, the love of siblings for each other when circumstances force them to bond together in their quest for unconditional love. I feel perfectly safe in saying that our grandparents gave us unconditional love while our parents offered a conditional one, a love which could and did change at their slightest whim. That kind of love definitely was what we neither sought nor needed. Yet I staunchly believe that out of the desperation in which we sought their love, we gained a strength we might not otherwise have developed, for the *ability* to love was never eradicated in us: we simply had to choose more carefully those to whom we gave our love. This, then, forged us into the survivors we both became.

Look, read, ponder, and you will understand.

Selah! And A-men!

THE EMPTY STAGE

The stage boards creak,
But no one strides
Across them.
Velvet curtains droop,
Hang motionless,
From ropes that sag and sway.

Black darkness fills the room,
Every mote-filled seat is empty.
Neither spotlight nor floodlight
Pierce the gloom,
For he is gone,
And the theater is
In mourning.

Shirley Gordon Jackson

Photograph of Charles Gordone, which accompanied the August 28, 1988, article "Seeking 'True American Theater'." Copyrighted material used by permission of *The Truth*.

NOTES

1. Parrish, Charles H. "Table II: Notions about Color Groups as Revealed by 400 Subjects" in "Color Names and Color Notions," *Journal of Negro Education* 15, no. 1 (1946): 13–20.

2. Loving, Jerome. *Walt Whitman: The Song of Myself.* Los Angeles: University of California Press, 1999. Preface, xiv.

3. Ramsey, Buck. "Anthem." From *And as I Rode Out on the Morning.* Lubbock, Texas: Texas Tech University Press, 1993.

INDEX

Page numbers in *italics* refer to illustrations